Microsoft® Office Documen
Your Easy-to-Use Toolkit an
How-To Source for Professi
Documents

PUBLISHED BY
Microsoft Press
A Division of Microsoft Corporation
One Microsoft Way
Redmond, Washington 98052-6399

Library of Congress Cataloging-in-Publication Data pending.

Printed and bound in the United States of America.

1 2 3 4 5 6 7 8 9   QWT   9 8 7 6 5 4

Distributed in Canada by H.B. Fenn and Company Ltd.

A CIP catalogue record for this book is available from the British Library.

Microsoft Press books are available through booksellers and distributors worldwide. For further information about international editions, contact your local Microsoft Corporation office or contact Microsoft Press International directly at fax (425) 936-7329. Visit our Web site at www.microsoft.com/learning/. Send comments to *mspinput@microsoft.com*.

Acquisitions Editor: Alex Blanton
Developmental and Project Editor: Sandra Haynes
Technical Editor: Jim Johnson
Copyeditor: Brenda Pittsley
Indexers: Patricia Masserman and Shawn Peck

Body Part No. X10-46137

To Mom and Dad, for always being there.

I cannot fix on the hour, or the spot, or the look, or the words which laid the foundation. It is too long ago. I was in the middle before I knew that I had begun.

—Jane Austen in the voice of Mark Darcy, *Pride and Prejudice*

Table of Contents

See how you can save time and make the time you spend in Office more productive, regardless of how simple or complex a document you need.

What do you think of this book?
We want to hear from you!

Microsoft is interested in hearing your feedback about this publication so we can continually improve our books and learning resources for you. To participate in a brief online survey, please visit: *www.microsoft.com/learning/booksurvey/*

Check out the essential principles-the *rules* of Word, Excel, and PowerPoint, if you will-that can simplify and beautify every document you create.

Create great documents with nothing more than the core building blocks available in Word, and discover the essential elements for almost any document you create.

Incorporate Excel charts to slim down and punch up your pages, and see how Excel can show you the most effective way to present your particular data.

Use PowerPoint to get your readers to notice exactly what you want them to see-and check out how to bring the best elements of Word, Excel, and PowerPoint together in your document.

Use Word, Excel, and PowerPoint to help you communicate effectively and create your own brand image for a consistent, professional, unique statement in every document.

Focus on what you can do in creating your document to make the most effective statement on the page-simply, efficiently, and professionally-and make it distinctly yours, right down to the footnotes!

What do you think of this book? We want to hear from you!	Microsoft is interested in hearing your feedback about this publication so we can continually improve our books and learning resources for you. To participate in a brief online survey, please visit: *www.microsoft.com/learning/booksurvey/*

Acknowledgments

It's nearly impossible to express how fortunate I feel for having the opportunity to work with a company and a group of people like Microsoft Learning. This project has been a phenomenal trip! Thank you for taking it with me. In particular:

- Sandra Haynes, MODD's developmental and project editor (metaeditor, really!) and partner in crime. You are the greatest gift any author could imagine! MODD is as much yours as it is mine. Thank you.

- Alex Blanton, acquisitions editor and MODD's tireless champion. Thank you for believing in me and in this project and for always being so good to the both of us!

- Josh Barnhill, product manager and my hero. Thank you for your patience and for every effort.

- Infinite thanks to the other amazing members of the MODD squad: Patricia Bradbury, Carl Diltz, Jim Johnson, Jim Kramer, Robert Lyon, Patty Masserman, Joel Panchot, Shawn Peck, Leslie Phillips, Brenda Pittsley, Julia Stasio, Debbie Swanson, Bill Teel, and all of the designers, production staff, software testers, and everyone who worked on this project!

Outside of Microsoft, many thanks are also warranted. To Lesa O'Daniel and Tim John, for helping me fix the compass that directed me here. To Tanya Woods, Tish Gilvey, Alex Jennings, and all of my clients, for your patience and support. To Elise, Michael, Ari, and Jared, for believing that I still exist without physical proof. And, to Fin and Janie, never last or least, for my sanity and my joy.

Introducing the Microsoft Office Document Designer!

The document shown below contains 21 graphic objects and 18 tables. The file size of this document is 153 KB. Was it created by a graphic designer? Using professional graphic design tools? At a print shop? Nope. This document was created in Microsoft Office Word 2003 using nothing but applications from the Office System. Unbelievable? No smoke and mirrors here; check it out for yourself. Once you've installed the tools on the Microsoft Office Document Designer (also known as MODD) CD, open this document, named *Believe it or not.doc*, from your *MODD Samples* folder. Then, play with it: edit it, print it, e-mail it anywhere. Do with it as you please. It's perfectly stable. This document has no fear. This is what Office can really do.

1. It's all about the documents!
2. Save time and get incredible results
3. Find all the help you need **4.** It's much easier than you think **5.** Let Office amaze you!

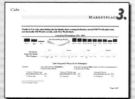

What's the best thing about this document? It's so much easier to create than anyone would imagine. That's where this book and the MODD tools come in. The next chapter will give you a detailed look at how the document was created and provide more information about how MODD can help you do everything you see. But before we go farther, let me provide some quick answers about the who, what, when, where, and why of the Microsoft Office Document Designer.

What's Inside

MODD is not your traditional computer book. It's a hands-on, practical set of tools that can teach you the techniques you need to know to create impressive, powerful documents with Office. And, in many cases, MODD can do the work for you.

MODD is not a general reference to the Office System, however. You won't find information about sending e-mail in Microsoft Outlook, building forms in Microsoft InfoPath, or creating slide presentations in Microsoft PowerPoint. MODD is all about creating documents. Here's what you will find inside:

- On the accompanying CD, you'll find the MODD tool, which consists of seven toolbars for Word, Excel, and PowerPoint that automate both complex and repetitive tasks, and help you take full advantage of the features these applications have to offer.

- Several hundred pages of objective tip sheets and thorough but brief instructional articles (electronic and printable!) covering a wide range of Word, Excel, and PowerPoint document production features. Access these articles and tip sheets from the *How Do I...* button on the MODD toolbars in each of the three applications.

■ This concise and information-packed *Design Guide* for quick reference to the MODD tool. This *Design Guide* is also a creative helping hand for making amazing documents, whether you need a presentation to impress your largest client, a report that will knock their socks off, or a professional brand image on every letter and memo you write.

Who Is This Book and CD Kit For?

The tool, articles, and tips you'll find in the Microsoft Office Document Designer (MODD) were created for people who use the document production features in Word, Excel, and PowerPoint. They're for Office users who want to push the envelope with Office but want it to be easier at the same time; who want to take full advantage of everything the applications have to offer; and who want to stretch the boundaries and create incredible documents. Whew! MODD is also for those who already know their way comfortably around Office and simply want to spend less time getting things done. Whether you need to quickly create presentations that impress, reports that make your point perfectly with your own custom design, or just everyday memos and letters that include your company logo, MODD will help you spend less time on your documents and deliver incredible results.

How can MODD help? For starters, let's take a look at a few possibly startling things you might not know about your documents:

■ Every time you press Enter on your keyboard, you add another set of formatting to your Word document. (Why is this important? You'll be amazed at the difference it makes! See the *How Do I...* tip sheet "Strong to the Core! Paragraph Formatting Essentials for Unbreakable Documents" for more information, and use the designs in the MODD tool for simple-to-apply, great-looking text layout.)

- When you embed an Excel chart in your Word document, anyone who opens that document can access not just your chart, but *all* the data on *every* sheet of the Excel workbook from which you got the chart. (Can you avoid that? Of course! See the *How Do I...* tip sheet "Getting Your Excel, PowerPoint or Any Objects into Word," and then let the MODD tool size *and* copy that chart to Word for you.)

- When you e-mail or otherwise share your documents electronically, you might be giving the recipient access to every edit you've ever made in the document—for example, if you copied and changed a presentation from one you made last year for another client. How's that for an "oops"?! (So is it bad to e-mail documents? Not at all! See the *How Do I...* tip sheet "Do You Really Know Your Documents? Managing Document Privacy: The Lowdown on Metadata" and use the MODD tool's metadata cleaner to help remove private information before you share your documents.)

- Just because a document looks okay when you print it, doesn't mean it will look the same on the other end when you e-mail it! (You gotta be kidding? Nope, afraid not. But follow a few simple rules in your documents and this will never happen to you! The *How Do I...* tip sheet "Making Your Word Documents Behave" will help ensure that what you see is what they get, and the many flexible layouts available in the MODD tool can create stable, manageable layouts in literally *seconds*—for the best looking documents you've ever sent anywhere!)

If making documents in Office has felt overcomplicated in the past, you're not alone. Many companies pile application on top of application to help Office do the things they need, little realizing that Office could do a better job all by itself! In fact, the MODD tool was built using *nothing* but the applications of the Office System. Complex documents don't have to mean complicated work. Ironically, the key to making Office do virtually everything you want it to is using the simplest methods possible. That's the MODD theme: the less work you do, the better your documents will be.

MODD is equally useful for those with more or less experience creating Office documents; however, it's not the best choice for the total beginner. While you can find basic information on using Excel and PowerPoint elements in your documents, you'll get the best results from MODD if you already have some experience using Word.

What About System Requirements?

The Microsoft Office Document Designer is designed for the Office System and also supports Office XP. To install and successfully use the MODD tool, here are the minimum requirements:

- Computer and processor: A personal computer with an Intel Pentium III or faster processor is recommended

- Memory: 256 MB RAM or greater is recommended

- Hard disk: 40 MB of available hard-disk space

- Drive: CD-ROM or DVD drive

- Monitor: Super VGA (800 x 600) or higher-resolution monitor

- Software Applications: Office 2003 or Office XP

- Operating System: Windows 2000, Windows XP, or later

Important You'll get the most benefit from MODD when you're running Word, Excel, and PowerPoint. However, as long as you are running Word, you can install the MODD tools for just those applications that are available on your computer. Please keep in mind, however, that the MODD tool does not support versions of *any* Office application earlier than Office XP.

Please note that computers with processors slower than Intel Pentium III or with less system memory than 256MB of RAM may experience a lag when running some of the MODD macros.

For best results, in addition to the system requirements listed here, you might want to prepare something to do with the time you're going to save using these tools. Whether that's calling more clients, inventing the world's next great innovation, winning a Nobel Prize, going out with friends, playing with your cat, reading a book, or taking a nap is entirely up to you!

Sounds Great, But When Am I Really Gonna Use This?

You don't need another book to answer one or two questions and then sit on a shelf until it becomes obsolete. MODD is not about showing off the bells and whistles of the software just because they look cool or sound easy. It's not some theoretical reference from an instructor who's never had to create a document. This is a real-world, practical tool written by a real-world, hands-on document expert. If it's taught, recommended, or automated in any component of MODD, I've used it and I know it works. You'll find answers about the stuff that never seems to work the way you want it to, and the reasons why one method or another is the best choice for what you need to accomplish.

This tool is the product of nine years of Office document production experience in high-pressure, highly competitive, professional environments. Even after you've learned what you need to know from MODD, continue to use it on every document, every day, so that you spend less time in Office and more time on whatever it is you want to do.

Excellent! Now Show Me What I Can Create with Office!

That's exactly what the next chapter is going to do.

First, the pages that immediately follow will help you install and get started using the MODD tool, and give you a quick and easy reference to what you'll find in each component.

Installing MODD

Installing the MODD tool couldn't be easier!

1. Close all Microsoft Office applications (including Outlook) and insert the enclosed CD into your computer's CD drive. A start window should appear automatically. If not, browse to your CD drive and double-click *StartCD.exe*.

2. In the start window, click the option to Install Microsoft Office Document Designer, and follow the brief instructions provided there to access the installation wizard.

3. As installation begins, you will be prompted to enter an installation ID in order to proceed. Type the eight characters that follow exactly as they appear here and then click Next to proceed:

   FNBXJNME

4. Follow the installation wizard and proceed as directed in the dialog boxes that appear.

   The MODD tools will automatically install for Word, Excel, and/or PowerPoint, depending on which of these applications are available on your system.

Important   Prior to running the installation CD, open Word and select Tools, Macro, Security. In that dialog box, set macro security to Medium. Then, repeat this exact step in Excel and PowerPoint.

When you set macro security to Medium, you will still be prompted before files containing macros can be opened. However, if you prefer higher macro security, you can increase the security level once the MODD tool is installed and running in all applications.

7

Here are a few additional notes to help with installation and setup:

- The tools will *not* install if your versions of Word, Excel, or PowerPoint are earlier than 2002 (Office XP), or if Word is not installed on your computer.

- All MODD sample files will be installed to a subfolder in your My Documents folder named *MODD Samples*.

- In order for the MODD tools and *How Do I...* articles and tip sheets to be accessible and function properly, please do *not* move any MODD files (other than those you create) from their original locations.

- If you experience any trouble with installation or error messages when you first use the MODD tools, check out the Troubleshooting section at the back of this *Design Guide*.

- When you next open Word, you will be greeted by a Welcome note advising you to set up your preferences in the My Options dialog box. An introduction to My Options is included in Getting Started in this chapter.

  If you choose not to enter your preferences right away in My Options, you will continue to be greeted with the Welcome note each time you start Word until you do so.

  However, it is *not* necessary to provide any information you don't want to include in My Options. The only required contact information is your name, as you would like it to appear in applicable documents.

The MODD tools are now ready to go! Check out the Getting Started section that follows for a quick introduction to each of the MODD toolbars.

Getting Started

A quick overview of each of the seven MODD toolbars follows, as well as more detail on how to find the answers you need in *How Do I...* and how to use this *Design Guide*.

The MODD Toolbars for Word

The MODD Main toolbar is the place to start in Word! Click the Get Started button for more details on each option available from the MODD toolbars in Word and set your preferences in the My Options dialog box (including such things as contact information you'd like MODD to include in your documents, setting up a logo to add to your documents, and selecting preferences for how the MODD tools appear and function).

Create a Doc is the button to select to start any new document—including a letter, memo, fax, presentation, or report, or even a new blank document that gives you access to all the MODD tools.

Click the How Do I... button for access to all *How Do I...* articles and tip sheets. See a quick overview of what to expect from *How Do I...* later in this chapter.

The MODD Design and Layout toolbar gives you access to applying and customizing all of the available MODD designs and layouts you will see later in the *Design Guide*. Apply a new design to an existing MODD document, insert a new layout, save or edit a custom design, or apply your design's colors to text, borders, and shading throughout your documents.

Note The features available on the MODD Design And Layout toolbar, as well as some of the features on other MODD toolbars in Word, are available only in documents you create using Create a Doc on the MODD Main toolbar. Keep in mind that you can create a blank MODD document when you want to start your own document from scratch, and still have those tools available for whenever you might need them.

The MODD Doc Tools toolbar provides a number of supporting tools for use with any MODD document. Here's a bit about what you can do:

- **Metadata Tools**   Check your document for many types of hidden data and remove content you don't want others to see. (Can be used in any document, regardless of whether it was created with the MODD tools.)

- **Table Formatting Tools**   One-click access to formatting your Word tables.

- **Presentation Tools**   Insert several pages at once with styles and layouts already set, add a table of contents page, or get help for managing headers and footers.

- **Shapes and Objects**   Insert accent shapes that match your document's design, add your saved logo wherever you like, or get help managing the shapes and objects in your document. (Can be used in any document, regardless of whether it was created with the MODD tools.)

- **Outline Numbering**   One-click access to starting an outline numbered list or using paragraph-numbering fields in your document.

The MODD Toolbars for Excel

The MODD Excel Design Tools toolbar gives you the options to apply design colors from any MODD design (both pre-created designs and those you customize)

to the font, borders, lines, and fill of worksheet elements or charts, as well as help sizing your charts and placing them in your Word document, and help creating charts from pivot tables.

The MODD Excel Workbook Tools toolbar helps you locate and resolve several types of hidden content in your Excel workbooks and provides access to the *How Do I...* tip sheets and articles. Notice that you also have a Get Started option on this toolbar, which provides more detail about the features available from both of the MODD Excel toolbars.

The MODD Toolbars for PowerPoint

The MODD PowerPoint Design Tools toolbar gives you the options to apply design colors from any MODD design (both pre-created designs and those you customize) to the text, lines, and fill of shapes and objects, as well as help sizing your objects and placing them in your Word document.

The MODD PowerPoint Support Tools toolbar helps you locate and resolve many types of hidden content in your PowerPoint file and provides access to the *How Do I...* tip sheets and articles. Notice that you also have a Get Started option on this toolbar, which provides more detail about the features available from both of the MODD PowerPoint toolbars.

Find the Answers in *How Do I...*

How Do I... is the place to find practical, complete answers to almost any Word, Excel, or PowerPoint document production question. *How Do I...* tip sheets and articles can be found by clicking the How Do I... button on the appropriate MODD toolbar in Word, Excel, and PowerPoint.

The *How Do I...* tip sheets provide quick reference information on both basic and advanced Word, Excel, and PowerPoint document production tasks. Use them for help in determining a best practice (such as how to indent text), solving a problem (such as understanding what an error message means and what to do about it), and in many cases getting start-to-finish instructions for executing tasks (such as creating headers and footers) along with key tips for keeping the task simple and manageable.

The *How Do I...* articles are complete, start-to-finish tasks covering a host of topics—from core stuff (such as creating paragraph styles) to advanced tasks (such as creating nested tables in Word or sizing Excel charts). Every article explains when and why to use the feature, and though there might be some setup required (just like gathering the ingredients for a great recipe), no *How Do I...* article task takes more than three steps to execute! The articles always use the method that gets the best results with the least work. Yup—outline-numbered lists, customized fields, even PivotTables, executed in *three steps or less*.

All *How Do I...* documents will open in your Web browser and can be printed for easy reference. Find an index to all *How Do I...* topics at the back of this *Design Guide*.

Note All references to tip sheets or articles throughout MODD refer to *How Do I...* articles and tip sheets.

How The *Design Guide* Can Help

So how about this *Design Guide*? As you move on to the next chapter, we'll take a closer look at the sample document shown at the beginning of this chapter and start talking about ways to save you time when you create documents. Then, in Chapter 02, I'll give you an introduction to the core underlying concepts of how Word, Excel, and PowerPoint think, so you can focus on being creative instead of on how to make features work.

Design Guide Chapters 03 through 07 offer sample document projects that showcase the available MODD designs and layouts. These projects offer tips and recommendations throughout for creating extraordinary documents with ease or making an extraordinary impact with even the simplest document. *After all, it's not about the document, it's about the statement the document helps you make!*

Follow along and try the projects for yourself or even check out the completed project documents, which are all available in your *MODD Samples* folder.

Now, are you ready to start creating brilliant documents? Let's go!

Incredible Documents, Incredibly Easy:
What you can do with the Microsoft Office System will amaze you!

You want to create extraordinary documents with ease, and you have less time than ever to get them done. It is the twenty-first century, after all. Everything today is faster, brighter, more colorful, more portable, more powerful. Why shouldn't you be able to say the same about your documents?

Take a look at Word, the place where your documents are born. There appears to be a myriad ways to perform almost any task, but the fact is there's a best way to do almost everything. Workarounds and "fudging it" always take more effort and time than doing it right, and the results often leave you frustrated. Instead, use

1. *Your document's possibilities*
2. *Flexible, creative options*   *3.* *Serious shortcuts*   *4.* *Less time in, better results out*

the software the way it's designed to be used, and you'll be amazed at how easy everything becomes! You'll create documents with no stress that are every bit as stable and manageable as they are beautiful, and it will take less time than you've ever spent on a document before.

Important   Nested tables, shown in the diagrams that follow, is the Word feature that makes the sample document so simple to create. See the article "Never Leave the Nest! Nesting Tables Is the Simple Solution to Amazing Documents" for step-by-step, no-nonsense instructions that show you how easy that feature really is.

Let's take a hands-on look at one example. The diagrams that follow take a closer look at the document you saw in the introduction, to show you just what *you* can do with Office.

See Also: As mentioned earlier, if you've installed the MODD tool, you can open and examine a live copy of the sample document for yourself. Find the document (named *Believe it or not.doc*) in your *MODD Samples* folder. In the same folder, find supporting Excel and Power-Point files with the same name that contain all the graphics you'll see in this document.

While you look at the sample document, let's talk about how to start saving time and making the time you spend in Office more productive, regardless of how simple or complex the document you need.

Total time to design, format and layout everything on this page: 42 minutes.

I used the MODD tools to help design and format the document in Word, including the design colors, layout, paragraph styles and table formatting...

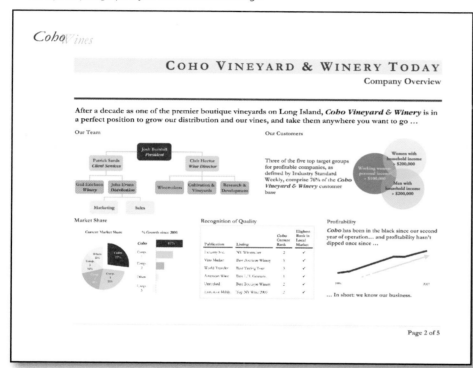

Word, Excel and PowerPoint features used to create this page: (Find help on every feature listed on these pages in How Do I):

Word

- Font formatting
- Paragraph formatting
- Paragraph styles
- Tables
- Headers & footers
- Page numbering
- Pasting pictures

PowerPoint

- AutoShapes
- Duplicating shapes
- Draw menu tools

Excel

- Bar charts
- Pie charts
- Line charts
- AutoShapes
- Formulas

...and to help format and place the Excel and PowerPoint elements you see throughout this document.

Total time to design, format and layout everything on this page: 33 minutes

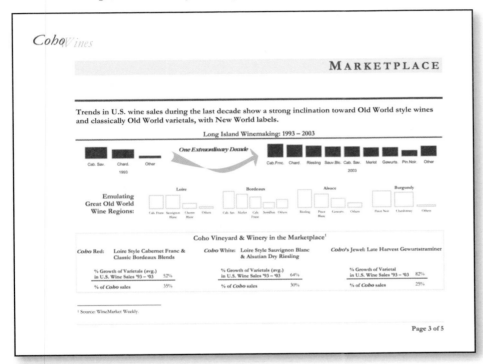

When I watch people working in Word, Excel, or PowerPoint, one of the most distressing things I see (and it happens all the time!) is what I call typewriter syndrome. Something seems to go wrong, you get frustrated, so you start *all over again*. Sound familiar? If it does, you're in good company. I've seen attorneys, secretaries, bankers, even document production specialists do the same thing! The good news is you're not working on a typewriter! You don't have to trash that page and roll a new sheet of paper into the carriage. All you need is Edit, Undo.

Total time to design, format and layout everything on this page: 40 minutes

Additional Word and Excel features used this page:

Word

• Bullets and numbering

Excel

• Area charts
• Combination chart types
• Multi-axis charts

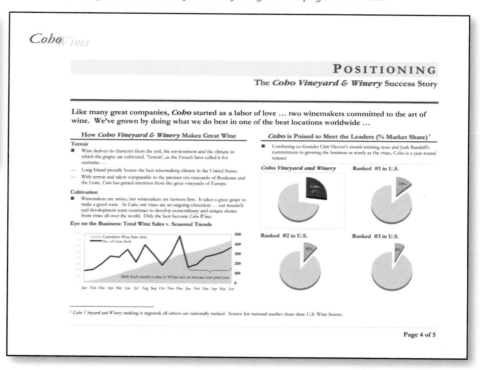

Total time to design, format and layout everything on this page: 32 minutes

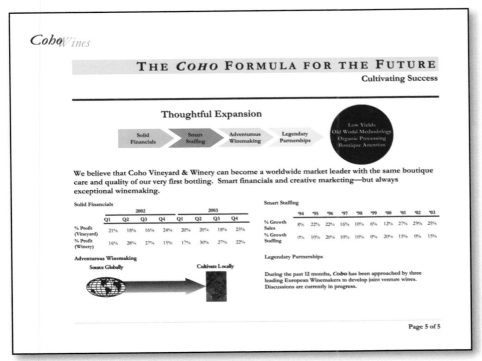

Additional PowerPoint features used this page:

- Inserting pictures
- Recoloring pictures
- Editing clip art

■ Did you know that, depending on what actions you've taken, Word can undo up to your last 300 steps? PowerPoint can undo up to the last 150 actions. And, Excel, while undoing what sounds like a comparably small 16 actions—can get you out of most any jam so you don't waste your time redoing things that were just fine to begin with!

To undo your last action, just press Ctrl+**Z** on your keyboard (this takes you back one step at a time) until you like what you see. If you go back too far, Ctrl+**Y** will redo your undone actions one at a time. Prefer the mouse? Just click the Undo or Redo arrows on the Standard toolbar, as shown here:

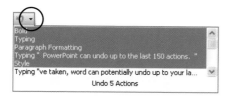

Or select Undo or Redo as needed from the Edit menu. And, to undo or redo several actions at a time, click the drop-down arrow beside the undo or redo toolbar buttons (as you see below) and drag your mouse down the list to select as many items as you want to undo (or redo).

Never do extra work again!

Note In Excel and PowerPoint, undo and redo options are cleared each time you save the file, as well as each time Excel or PowerPoint executes an AutoRecover save.

How about a few more timesavers? Here are some favorites I can't do without:

■ Ever spend more time than you'd care to admit trying to figure out what formatting is applied to text, a paragraph, or a page in your Word document? Try this instead: place your insertion point in the text you want to investigate, then press Shift+**F1** to open the Reveal Formatting task pane, where you'll see the applied Font, Paragraph, Bullets And Numbering, Table, and even Section formatting all at a glance! What's more, each type of formatting listed in that task pane has a hyperlink to the correct dialog box needed to change the setting. For example, click Spacing, as shown here to open the Paragraph dialog box, where you can change line or paragraph spacing:

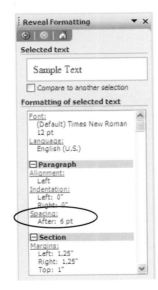

See Also: The tip sheet "The Long Document Heroes!" offers a closer look at the Reveal Formatting task pane.

- Ever apply formatting to one piece of text and then realize you need to do the same thing in a dozen different places in the document—or in other documents? Maybe you need the same text to repeat in every cell of a table column? Don't type it all again! Just press the **F4** key. **F4** repeats your last action *as many times as you like*, whether it's typing or formatting, in the same or other open documents until you perform another action or exit Word. F4 works in PowerPoint as well, and it even works in Excel for text and chart formatting.

- You might already know that you can bold (Ctrl+**B**), change paragraph alignment (Ctrl+**L** for left, **E** for center, **R** for right, and **J** for justified), or copy text (Ctrl+**C**) with just a keystroke, but how about this: clear all font formatting (such as italics, 15 point, Arial font) that's not part of the selection's paragraph style in one step by pressing Ctrl+Spacebar. (Ctrl+**Q** does the same for direct paragraph formatting.)

See Also: Not sure of the difference between formatting in a paragraph style and *direct* formatting? There's a set of articles and tip sheets covering everything you need to know about paragraph styles that you'll definitely want to check out. Styles are a key Word feature for making beautiful, stress-free documents!

See Also: For help with any of the shortcuts listed here, as well as a thorough list of the most helpful shortcut keystrokes in Word, Excel, and PowerPoint, check out the tip sheet "Shortcuts!"

Well, you might be thinking that all these shortcuts still won't get you to a document like the one you see diagrammed here. Actually, the shortcuts aren't a bad way to start. But more important is the fact that most features that look complicated on these pages are far simpler than you think.

Tip   To add font formatting to a single word, just click in the word (no need to select it) and apply your formatting, such as Ctrl+**I** for italics or Ctrl+**U** for underline. Or select the text to apply font formatting to more or less than one word at a time. For paragraph formats, just click in a single paragraph and apply formatting, such as Ctrl+**M** to indent the paragraph or Ctrl+**2** to apply double line spacing. You can also select several paragraphs to format them all at once.

Note   If clicking into a word to apply character formatting (rather than selecting the word) doesn't work for you, go to Tools, Options, Edit and select the option When selecting, automatically select entire word.

Let's look, for example, at the organization chart on the first page of the sample document. Don't like the rounded rectangles? No problem! Just select the whole chart in PowerPoint and then select Change AutoShape from the Draw menu.

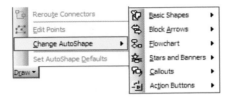

Pick a new shape—try the oval from the Basic Shapes menu or a starburst from Stars and Banners. With that one action, PowerPoint will change all of the rounded rectangles to the shape you select, while leaving your formatting and the connector lines intact. Sound too easy to be true? Try it for yourself. Open *Believe it or not.ppt* and test it on the exact organization chart you see here. Or for more detailed help working with shapes, see the PowerPoint tip sheet "The Essentials of a Good Figure: Working with Shapes."

Now, that's easy!

Regardless of what you need from your documents, it's likely that there's an Office solution as efficient as those you've seen on the preceding pages. The next chapter of this *Design Guide* will introduce you to some essential, underlying principles for making your work with Word, Excel, and PowerPoint as efficient and effective as possible. From there, try out (or just check out) the document projects in subsequent chapters, for Office documents that will surprise and delight you!

Chapter Summary

The Office System is a powerful set of applications. No one book could teach you everything you can do with them. No class could cover it all. And if it could, who would have the time? Instead, understand the core principles and you'll have the comfort and confidence to take on any new task for yourself.

MODD's goal is to help you make incredible documents, by making the most of your time with Microsoft Office: minimum time in, maximum results out.

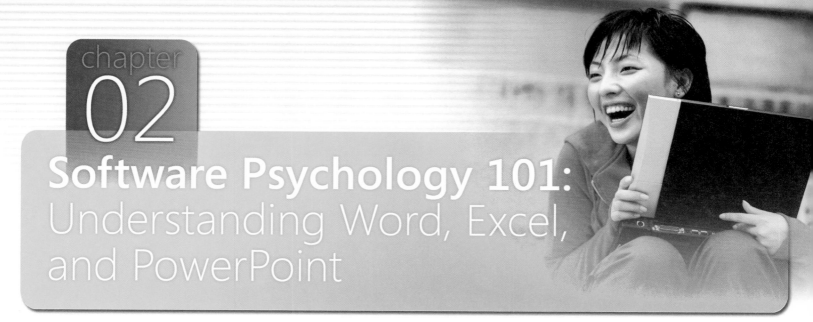

chapter 02

Software Psychology 101:
Understanding Word, Excel, and PowerPoint

Before we begin building documents, let's put a foundation in place. This chapter will look at the essential principles—the *rules* of Word, Excel, and PowerPoint, if you will—that can simplify and beautify every document you create.

One of the most common frustrations when trying to learn any software application is that no one tells you why to do anything. You get *click* this and *select* that, but why should you click this instead of that? Why is A a better solution than B when there are at least five ways to do what you're trying to accomplish? And, perhaps most important, what do you do after you've clicked and selected, and the results aren't what you expected?

1. Office's best practices   2. Time-saving approaches   3. Easy, great-looking graphics   4. Solid, beautiful documents

With Microsoft Office, when you understand some of the basics of how each application thinks, the answers to these questions fall into place. There is a reason for *everything* Word, Excel, and PowerPoint do, even though it might not seem that way at times.

For example, did you know that a single character of text, a paragraph mark (¶), and a section break

———————————————————Section Break (Next Page)———————————————————

all store formatting? If you've ever moved text from one place to another in Word and its formatting changed, or you did nothing more than press the Backspace key and everything went haywire, you can see why this information is important.

See Also: Get details on the three levels of Word formatting later in this chapter and find out what you need to know about how formatting is stored in your document.

This chapter will give you an overview of what makes Word, Excel, and Power-Point tick. We'll look at some core concepts behind Office document production in plain English, providing answers to the fundamental questions that connect the dots and turn isolated tasks into solid, stress-free documents.

Where Else Can Doing Less Get You Better Results?

Rule number one in the Office applications: if it feels like a lot work, you can be sure there's a better solution.

Word, Excel, and PowerPoint all work best when you do the least work possible for the task. In fact, they can get downright rebellious when you spend unnecessary time on convoluted workarounds. Let's look at a couple of examples where doing less work actually gives you better results:

- How would you expand the spacing of the word MEMORANDUM to match the document shown here?

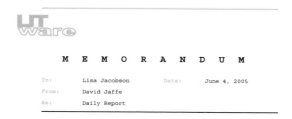

You might be inclined to take the old typewriter approach and type M...then five spaces...then E...then five spaces...and so on. Then, once you're done, 55 keystrokes later, you decide you want a little more space—you have to go back and add a space or two between each character, making sure to keep the number of spaces equal between all characters. All that for just one word! Do you really have that kind of time?

Tip As with many formatting commands throughout Office, Character Spacing is measured in *points*. Points are a typesetting standard unit of measure—72 points to an inch.

Tip The example word, MEMORANDUM, uses 25 points expanded spacing. For a faster solution than using the spin buttons to change the character spacing setting, try typing in the amount of points you think you want—the spin buttons change the number by only one-tenth of one point at a time. (Notice, however, that when you type in the amount of space, you'll need to tab or click in another text box in order to update the Preview at the bottom of the dialog box.)

A better solution is to select the word MEMORANDUM and then select Font from the Format menu. On the Character Spacing tab of the Font dialog box (shown below), select Expanded in the Spacing drop-down list and then set the amount of space you want in the By text box. Click OK when you like the result.

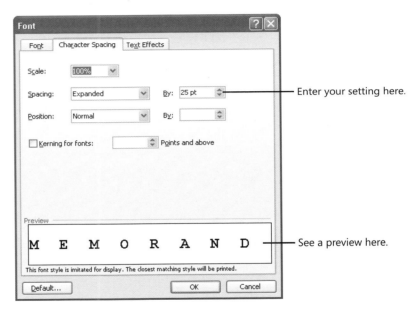

Enter your setting here.

See a preview here.

See Also: For more information on character formatting basics and best practices, including more details on the character spacing feature, check out the tip sheet "From Coloring to Paste: Tips and Tricks That Turn Editing Into Kid Stuff."

■ Okay, what if you needed to sum a few noncontiguous columns of numbers in an Excel spreadsheet, such as the quarterly totals in this sample data?

Q1 ($m)	% Change*	Q2 ($m)	% Change	Q3 ($m)	% Change	Q4 ($m)	% Change
$23	6.90%	$25	8.70%	$27	8.00%	$24	-11.11%
65	1.80%	64	-1.54%	62	-3.13%	64	3.23%
87	2.10%	82	-5.75%	85	3.66%	86	1.18%
54	-2.70%	59	9.26%	56	-5.08%	55	-1.79%
23	-4.00%	29	26.09%	28	-3.45%	22	-21.43%
23	3.20%	25	8.70%	26	4.00%	24	-7.69%
56	5.40%	58	3.57%	52	-10.34%	59	13.46%
32	-1.00%	28	-12.50%	36	28.57%	34	-5.56%
76	-1.60%	76	0.00%	73	-3.95%	75	2.74%
23	2.80%	26	13.04%	28	7.69%	28	0.00%

You could just start with an equal sign and then select each cell and type a plus sign between them—that doesn't sound like much work! But this relatively small data sample covers 40 worksheet cells, so it would take 80 keystrokes to create this formula, and just look at the results:

```
fx  =C4+C5+C6+C7+C8+C9+C10+C11+C12+C13+E4+E5+E6+E7+E8+E9+E10+E11+E12+E13+G4+G5+G6+
    G7+G8+G9+G10+G11+G12+G13+I4+I5+I6+I7+I8+I9+I10+I11+I12+I13
```

Try using the Sum function instead. Start the function by typing =SUM(. Then, hold down the **Ctrl** key (this allows you to select non-contiguous parts of the spreadsheet) while you drag to select the cells in each of the columns you need. When you're happy with your selection, press **Enter** to complete the formula, and this is what you'll get:

```
fx  =SUM(C4:C13,E4:E13,G4:G13,I4:I13)
```

Compare this formula to the earlier, workaround version with 40 separate cell references. Using the first version, how long would it take you to figure out you were missing one cell or had an incorrect entry in the formula? And what a headache it would be to edit if the cell ranges need to change! Instead, using a simple function that Excel provides, you can accomplish the task using a fraction of the time and effort and your results are both more dependable and easier to edit.

If the Office applications can save you that much time on simple tasks, imagine the time you'll save and the results you'll get using Office's best practices (that is, the tool designed for the task) throughout your documents! Of course, there is a catch: how do you know what's the best practice? Furthermore, with so many features available in more than one of the Office applications, how do you even know whether to use Word, Excel, or PowerPoint for whatever it is you need to do? The answer is much easier than you might think.

Let Each Application Do What It Does Best

"Dress sharply and they notice the dress; dress impeccably and they notice the woman."

This famous quote from Coco Chanel is surely as true for men as it is for women. It's also true for your documents.

Adding pizzazz to your documents is great, but no one will give you their business or publish your paper because of the color of your font or the fact that your pie charts are 3-D. Remember that the idea behind professional, stylish packaging is to get your document's *content* noticed. When you use the best method for each task in your document, letting Word, Excel, and PowerPoint each handle their part, the document's construction will be impeccable and your content will shine through.

In the age of electronic documents, the recipients of your documents see more than just a printed page, they see the document on screen, as you created it. Take this report page, for example:

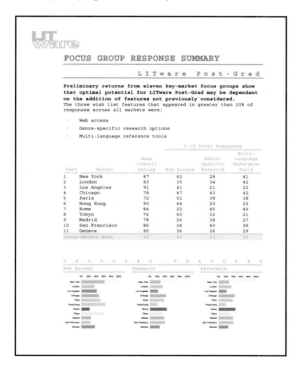

It's a clean, beautiful page that lets your information sparkle, right? Well, it might put a damper on your enthusiasm if you knew that the document on the left-hand side of the next page is what the recipient will actually see:

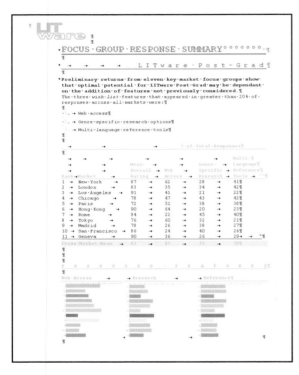

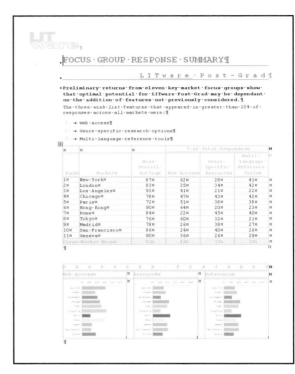

Perhaps more interesting is the fact that, using some common workarounds, it took more than three hours to create the page on the left. By contrast, using the best possible practices in Word and Excel, the version on the right took about half an hour to complete.

Note Formatting marks are nonprinting characters that show the spaces between words, tab characters, paragraph marks, etc. Learn more about working with formatting marks later in this chapter.

Formatting marks are shown in both versions. The document on the left looks so dreadful because of the way it was created. You might be thinking that your documents would never look like that because you don't turn on formatting marks—yet anyone on the receiving end of your documents surely can turn them on. Even if you protect the document, your recipients can still see the way it was created, and they'll still have to wade through that mess to get to your content.

Using the best practices in the sample on the right (such as a single Word table instead of a mass of tabs or one indent instead of several spaces), the page took about one-sixth of the time to create and looks infinitely better on screen. What's more, as you can easily tell by comparing these samples, it will also be much faster and less stressful to edit. So, before you think about the layout, colors, or graphics that make a document dazzle, take a look at some underlying principles that help you find the easy, fast, and all-around best solutions for every document task.

See Also: Open the well-built version of this sample report page and examine it for yourself. You'll find it in your *MODD Samples* folder, named *Chapter 02 Report Page.doc*.

Word—Where Document Production Lives

Word is the heart and soul of Office document production. It's the best place to build your documents—any documents. Even when you need to display financial data, you get far more formatting options in a Word table than you do in an Excel worksheet. And when you're creating a presentation that you plan to deliver on paper (whether printed or sent electronically), Word gives you much more power and flexibility than PowerPoint.

At the same time, though Word offers a handful of formulas and has built-in charting tools, they're nothing like Excel's frankly phenomenal number-crunching and charting capabilities. Likewise, notwithstanding the easily accessible drawing tools in Word, you'll end up doing much less work if you create presentation graphics for your document in PowerPoint. And it's a cinch to get Excel and PowerPoint elements into your Word document—so using the strengths of each application will help save you time and stress.

See Also: Get help for all of the tasks mentioned in this chapter in the *How Do I...* articles and tip sheets. See the Index to How Do I... Content at the back of this *Design Guide* for a reference to all topics covered.

Understanding How Word Thinks Can Eliminate 90 Percent of Your Document Production Stress

Since your documents live in Word, they'll have a much better time of things if they abide by the landlord's rules. Word is a great landlord—you can do pretty much whatever you want, provided you take care of the place and respect a few straightforward policies:

- **Use the feature that's designed for the task.** As demonstrated earlier in this chapter, workarounds take more time than using the feature that's designed for the task and the results are never as good. Even if you don't know which feature is the right feature, it usually takes less time to find it than to fudge it.

- **Save time by taking your time.** While that sounds like plain common sense, it's common to get into trouble in a document because something goes wrong and you just keep going. If you don't know why something happened in your document, or don't like the results of an action, undo it (**Ctrl+Z** or Edit, Undo) before you move on. After all, it's much easier to get that stain out of your carpet when the drink first spills than after you've been walking on it for a week!

- **Always watch what you're doing.** Word provides you with tools that enable you to stay in control of what's going on in the document. If you don't use them, you might be missing vital information.

  - **Formatting marks** As you saw in the sample report page earlier in this chapter, formatting marks let you see much of your document's formatting at a glance. Turn them on by clicking the paragraph mark icon on the Standard toolbar. Or you can turn them on by default for all documents by selecting your preferences on the View tab of the Tools, Options dialog box.

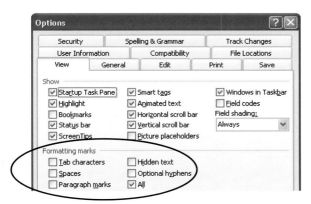

● **Views** Does it matter which view you use to work on your documents? It sure does! Normal view, for example, won't show you headers, footers, footnotes, or any page layout—but it uses less memory because of that, so it's great when you just need to edit text (particularly in long documents). Print Layout view uses more memory, but it shows you precisely what your document will look like—so it's usually the best choice when designing a layout or working with complex documents.

See Also: Find details on each view available to you in Word in the tip sheet "Making Your Word Documents Behave."

Now, with this short list of basic rules in mind, let's take a look at the core concepts behind everything you can do in Word.

A Quick Look at Word's Core Concepts

Perhaps the most enlightening piece of information I can give you about Word is to tell you that it's not really a word processing application. Instead, Word thinks like a *desktop publishing* application, considering a document's layout, design, and organization. Just the fact that the unit of measure for much Word formatting is a typesetting standard (i.e., points) tells you that this application is concerned with document layout, not just typing text.

Why is this important? Creating a document on a typewriter is linear—top to bottom. You start typing and format as you go. But formatting as you go in Word just doesn't work. Sure, you can *make* it work, but it will always be more complicated than necessary. Instead, you might say that Word does the opposite by looking at the document from the bottom to the top. More simply, Word looks at the whole page (the whole document, in fact) as a unit and organizes the formatting into manageable bites.

The Three Levels of Word Formatting

Most of the formatting you can apply in a Word document is organized into three levels: font, paragraph, and section. Let's take a look at what this means for you:

The Formatting Level	What It Controls	Where to Find It
Font formatting	Font formatting is the smallest, simplest level of formatting. It includes any formatting you can apply to as little as one character of text, including everything you access through Format, Font (such as font face, font style, font effects, character spacing, etc.), text borders and shading, and even the language setting.	All font formatting is stored directly in the character to which it's applied. See the font formatting stored in one sample character, as shown by the Reveal Formatting task pane (see Chapter 01 for an introduction to the Reveal Formatting task pane):

Reveal Formatting ▼ ×

Selected text

m

☐ Compare to another selection

Formatting of selected text

⊟ Font
Font:
(Default) Times New Roman
12 pt
Bold
Language:
English (U.S.)

sample

The Formatting Level	What It Controls	Where to Find It
Paragraph formatting	Paragraph formatting is anything you can do to as little as one paragraph, and that's most of the formatting your documents use. This includes everything in the Paragraph dialog box (Format, Paragraph), as well as paragraph borders and shading, bullets and numbering, and tab settings.	Paragraph formatting is stored in the paragraph mark that falls at the end of each paragraph. When you press Enter to start a new paragraph, the new paragraph mark contains the same formatting as the previous, until you change it. This helps your document's formatting remain more consistent. Take a look at a sample paragraph's formatting, as shown by the Reveal Formatting task pane:

The Formatting Level	What It Controls	Where to Find It
Section formatting	Section formatting is the third and largest level of formatting, and refers to what people often think of as page formatting. Section formatting includes everything you can apply to your document from the Page Setup dialog box (File, Page Setup), as well as headers and footers, text columns (for example, the Format, Columns command), some elements of document protection, and even the numbering of pages and footnotes.	Section formatting is stored in a Section Break (available from Insert, Break). See what the Reveal Formatting task pane has to say about Section formatting for a sample selection: Just as you need to press Enter for a new paragraph when you want to change paragraph formatting, you must insert a section break when you want to change any section-level formatting within a document.

See Also: Learn more about paragraph formatting in the tip sheet "Strong to the Core! Paragraph Formatting Essentials for Unbreakable Documents."

See the tip sheet "Document Essentials: Understanding Page (Section) Formatting" for more information on using Section formatting and a quick reference guide to all of the *How Do I...* Section formatting help topics.

Note   If tables seem to be conspicu-
ously missing from the three levels of formatting, it's because they aren't really
formatting. Tables are objects that organize content and its formatting, and they
can save you immeasurable time and
effort in almost any document. For help
getting started with tables, see the tip
sheet "The Greatest Document Tool Since
Paper! Introducing Word Tables." Find a
quick reference guide to all table topics
covered in *How Do I...* at the end of that
tip sheet.

What's the best way to make use of this information? Keep the three levels of formatting in mind to help you use the simplest method for any task, and avoid
adding unnecessary complications to your documents.

For example, if you need to indent two paragraphs of text, use paragraph indents
(Format, Paragraph, Indents And Spacing) rather than changing the page margins
for just that portion of one page. Changing margins requires section breaks
before and after the change, as well as the margin setting. Those section breaks
are two complete sets of formatting that you don't need and are sure to get in the
way—not to mention that the indents are faster and simpler to set, and can even
be stored in a paragraph style for quick, consistent application throughout your
document as needed.

Understanding the three levels of formatting helps you plan your documents so
that you spend as little time in them as possible. When you plan a document's
formatting, approach it from the outside in—that is, from the largest formatting
elements to the smallest. You'll end up doing the least work if you determine
what you need for section formatting first, followed by paragraph formatting,
and, finally, font formatting. That way, for example, if you need dozens of paragraphs with the same formatting, apply it all at once instead of in 20 or 30 separate steps. You'll do less work and leave less room for error.

Now, what about the elements in your document that aren't part of these three
levels of formatting, such as Excel charts or PowerPoint graphics? Let's take a look
at some best-practice essentials for Excel and PowerPoint to help save time and
improve your results in those applications as well.

Excel—Is There Anything It Can't Do With Numbers?!

Excel is my favorite software application for one reason: every time I've said it can't do something, I've been wrong. But because Excel has such power, it can be intimidating to new or occasional users. The ironic thing about Excel is that it's easier to use than Word because it doesn't have as many rules—if there's logic to it, Excel can do it.

If It's About Numbers, It Belongs Here!

When you need a table that looks elegant in your Word document, a Word table is the way to go. But when you need to actually crunch numbers for that table (such as calculating the percent change columns in the Excel worksheet earlier in this chapter), go to Excel and don't look back! Word formulas are limited—don't fuss and fight with them to try to get what you need. Copy and paste those numbers into Excel and let a few simple functions handle the work. It takes much less time to copy and paste between Excel and Word when you need number crunching *and* a great looking Word table than to try to force one or the other application to do things it's not meant to do.

> **See Also:** The tip sheet "The Old Switcheroo: Turning Excel Spreadsheets Into Word Tables and Vice Versa" for more detail on working between Excel spreadsheets and Word tables.

As for charts, there's a charting feature in both Word and PowerPoint, but neither has the power or flexibility of the charting functionality in Excel. You can do much more in less time with Excel charts because charts aren't a sidebar in Excel—they're a part of its primary tools.

The Pure and Simple Logic of Excel

The best way to stay in control with Excel is quite similar to the pointers about working in Word: save time by taking the time to use the correct feature for the task. And keep in mind that there is a simple reason and a simple solution even for those things that might look terrifying! For example, take a look at the chart that follows. Quite a mess, right? Actually, it's not a mess at all! The reason that pie is so tiny is because the default font size is too big for the plot area allotted in the chart.

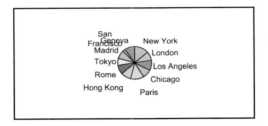

It takes just two steps to turn the chart into a chart you'd be happy to have in your report, as shown here:

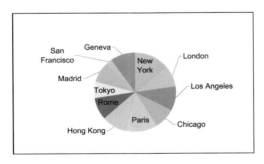

All I did was:

1. Drag the plot area to make it larger.
2. Move the data labels.

It took less than two minutes to fix.

> **See Also:** Get started with Excel charting using the tip sheet 'Chart Anatomy 101: Understanding Chart Elements and Selecting the Best Chart for Your Data' and check out the index at the end of this *Design Guide* for help on most Excel charting questions.

Just Because It's Powerful Software Doesn't Make It Hard!

Excel is very user friendly, if you allow it to be. Before you assume something's wrong, such as in the chart example, take a moment to look at it calmly and you're likely to see the simple solution.

Don't Like Math? That's a Great Reason to Get to Know Excel!

Countless times, I've heard Office users say they can't use Excel because they aren't good at math. The thing is, Excel does the math for you! When you need to insert a function or create a chart, read the dialog boxes as you go and you'll find a tremendous amount of help right in front of you. For example, if you need to use a mathematical function, start with the Insert Function dialog box, shown here:

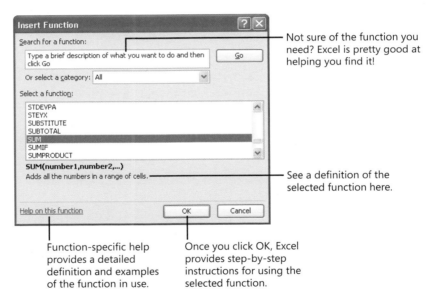

Not sure of the function you need? Excel is pretty good at helping you find it!

See a definition of the selected function here.

Function-specific help provides a detailed definition and examples of the function in use.

Once you click OK, Excel provides step-by-step instructions for using the selected function.

PowerPoint—Your Go-To Person for Presentation Graphics

Though Word has a Drawing toolbar, Word is not about graphics. When you create floating objects in Word (that is, graphics that float over the text of the document—as AutoShapes always do, for example), the document can become more difficult to manage. That doesn't mean you shouldn't add graphics to your document! It just means that you'll have a much easier time with your documents when you let PowerPoint do its part.

Of course you'd use PowerPoint to create slide shows, but it's also the place to go when you need presentation graphics for your Word documents. Organization charts, flow charts, and diagrams get more formatting options and are easier to manage if you create and store them in PowerPoint. (And keep in mind that the drawing toolbars in Word and PowerPoint are similar, so if you already know a bit about Word's drawing tools, you have a head start for using PowerPoint!)

If It's a Shape or Drawing You Need, This Is the Place to Do It!

Everything floats in PowerPoint! This application is specifically designed to let graphic objects do their thing. Just as you get more document formatting options when your document lives in Word, you'll get more formatting flexibility for presentation graphics when they're created in PowerPoint. And, as with Excel charts, it's quick and easy to get images of your PowerPoint objects into your Word documents—helping to keep your Word documents beautiful, stable, and easy to manage.

> **See Also:** Check out the article "Getting Your Excel, PowerPoint or Any Graphic Into Word" for help adding PowerPoint graphics to your Word documents.

Next Steps

Now that you know where to go for whatever document formatting task you might need, it's time to turn that information into better documents! The chapters that follow provide previews of the MODD designs and layouts, organized into sample document projects. Check them out for tons of document production tips, from managing Word tables to creating your own custom document designs. Follow along and try out the projects for yourself, or open and check out the finished products.

See Also: All sample documents shown in this *Design Guide* are available in the *MODD Samples* folder, which is saved to your My Documents folder when you install the MODD tool.

Keep in mind that the *How Do I...* articles and tip sheets available from within the MODD tools are there to help you with virtually any document production task. Use the index at the back of this *Design Guide* to find the topics you need, and use the MODD toolbars in Word, Excel, and PowerPoint to automate many of the tasks discussed in this and subsequent chapters.

See Also: Find quick reference tables to many of the concepts and standards presented in this chapter in the tip sheets "Making Your Word Documents Behave," "Making Your Excel Workbooks Behave," and "Making Your PowerPoint Objects Behave."

chapter 03

Impressing with Text:
Building basic presentation and report pages in Word

Essential, vital, central, principal, and straightforward—these are just some of the words offered by the Microsoft Office Research task pane as synonyms for the word *basic* as it's used in the title of this chapter. You're creating an important document. You have information you need to convey and you want it to be clearly understood and appreciated. Simply put, you want your document to make an impact.

A well-made, well-designed document helps your information shine through. And as discussed in the previous chapter, when it comes to building documents with the applications of Microsoft Office, a good document is easier and faster to create than the alternative!

1. *It's all about tables and styles!*
2. *Build solid Word pages* **3.** *Nest tables for flexibility* **4.** *Combine layouts* **5.** *Get creative with Word*

"The secret to being boring is to tell everything."
—Voltaire

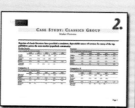
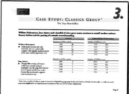

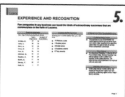

How Do I... Articles and Tip Sheets to Help with the Tasks in This Chapter

Topic	How Do I or Tip Sheet Title
Paragraph formatting	"Strong to the Core! Paragraph Formatting Essentials for Unbreakable Documents"
Styles	New to the Feature: "Introducing Styles: Understanding Paragraph, Character, List and Table Styles"
	More Experienced: "Managing Styles: Using the Styles And Formatting Task Pane"
Tables (general)	New to the Feature: "The Greatest Document Tool Since Paper! Introducing Word Tables!"
	More Experienced: "Essential Table Dos, Don'ts, and How Tos"
Nested tables	"Never Leave the Nest! Nesting Tables Is the Simple Solution to Amazing Documents"
Headers and footers	New to the Feature: "Document Essentials: Understanding Page (Section) Formatting"
	More Experienced: "Word Documents From Top to Bottom: Creating Headers and Footers That Work"

This chapter will take a look at building beautiful documents with nothing more than the core building blocks available in Word. These are the essential elements that can simplify almost any document you create, regardless of what goes into it. In a nutshell—it's all about *styles* and *tables*.

On the pages that follow, we'll look at three different design approaches to the same company's documents. From the most conservative, understated design to the utterly bold and brash, you'll see powerful pages that convey key information using nothing but Word.

Note that there is an exception to the statement that all content in this chapter's sample pages was created in Word. I used PowerPoint to create the three versions of our sample company's logo (as well as those logos you'll see in upcoming chapters). You'll find details about using PowerPoint to create logos in Chapter 05.

Building Great Text Pages

Perhaps you're thinking that you need bold graphics to get your point across clearly, like this:

Note Find the completed documents from this chapter in your *MODD Samples* folder, titled *Lucerne-Sales Report.doc*, *Lucerne-Case Study.doc*, and *Lucerne-Company Overview.doc*. To follow along and try the document projects for yourself, you may find it helpful to open and print a copy of the live, completed document for reference.

When creating the project documents yourself, find completed logos to insert into your documents in your *MODD Samples* folder. All logo files are named *Lucerne logo*—along with the color of the design they match (that is, *Lucerne logo – navy.emf, Lucerne logo – moss.emf, Lucerne logo – purple.emf* for this chapter's documents). The logos are saved either as *emf* or *tif* file types, the reasons for which are explained in Chapter 05.

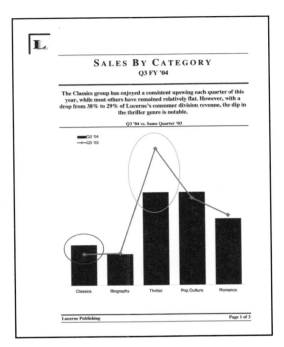

Sure, this is a great presentation page—points clearly made, key information powerfully expressed. We'll look at adding graphics like this in the chapters to come. But what about when you prefer not to use graphics? It's just as easy to make a compelling statement with clear, direct, visually accessible text. The good news is that going from point A to point B in the following example text page takes nothing more than a simple table and a handful of paragraph styles:

A　　　　　　　　　　　　　**B**

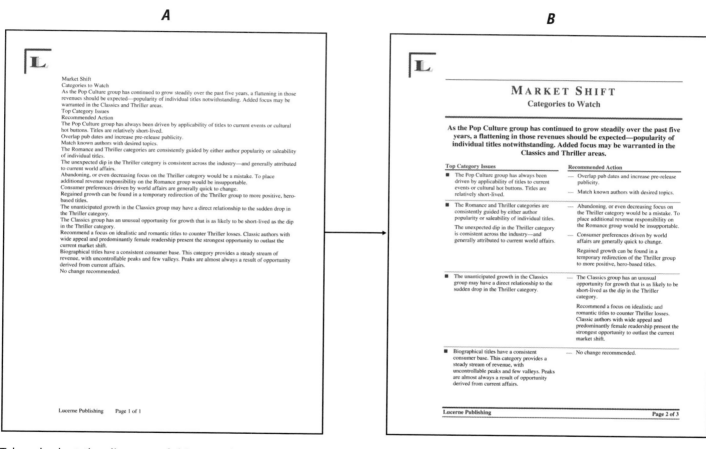

Take a look at the diagram of this completed page and how simply it was built:

This document is a Presentation/Report MODD document. The logo is saved through My Options (on the MODD Main toolbar) for automatic sizing and inclusion in your documents.

All but one of the paragraph styles you see on this page are part of the pre-created design (the custom style is the indented text below the bullets).

To get this look:

1. Click into the second row of the layout, go to Table, Table Properties, Row and deselect the Specify Height check box. That allows the row to be only as tall as your text requires.

2. Apply Bullet 1 style in the first column of the second row as you see at right, and Bullet 2 style in the third column (the second column is a divider column, used just to create space). When you've typed all the text you want for that row, press Tab from the third column to start a new row. Notice that the bulleted paragraph styles are automatically applied in the new row.

3. Select all cells of the second and third rows and apply horizontal cell borders between the two rows. This border is 1½ points thick, and uses the same blue as the design text, RGB(0,0,106). When you add more rows, they will automatically contain the same border between each.

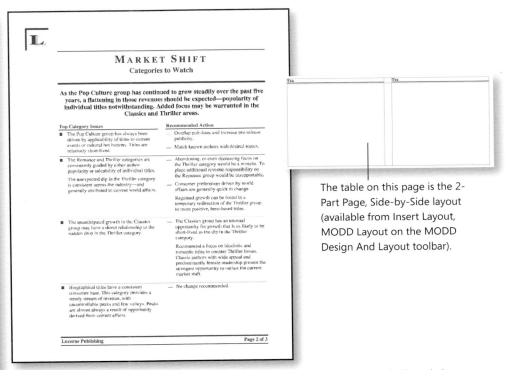

The table on this page is the 2-Part Page, Side-by-Side layout (available from Insert Layout, MODD Layout on the MODD Design And Layout toolbar).

By default, the footer style in this design is right-aligned. Change this footer to left-aligned, then place a right-aligned tab on the right margin. Type the company name on the left and then press the Tab key once in front of the page numbering to push it over to that right-aligned tab.

As you see, tables help to organize the page layout while styles organize the text within the layout. So what else can you do with just styles and tables? Let's take a look...

The next page contains text that obviously belongs in a table format (the bottom half of the page), as well as what you might think is a graphic of a flowchart (the top half of the page), but this page contains no graphic objects!

For the two tables you see on this page, you can start with the MODD Layout 2-Part Page, Top & Bottom and then split the layout into two parts (using Table, Split Table). But, you might prefer to create your own tables in this case.

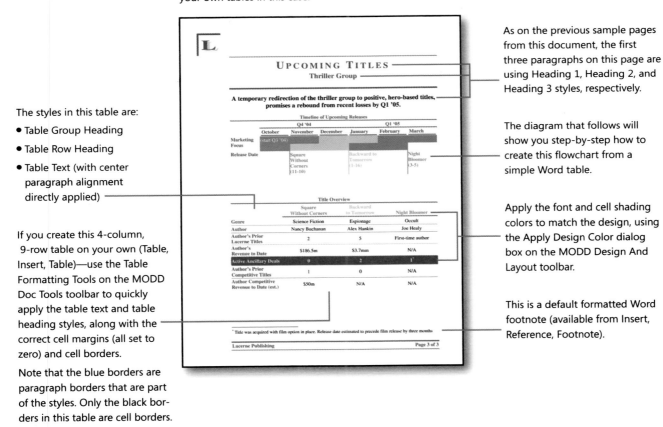

As on the previous sample pages from this document, the first three paragraphs on this page are using Heading 1, Heading 2, and Heading 3 styles, respectively.

The styles in this table are:

- Table Group Heading
- Table Row Heading
- Table Text (with center paragraph alignment directly applied)

The diagram that follows will show you step-by-step how to create this flowchart from a simple Word table.

If you create this 4-column, 9-row table on your own (Table, Insert, Table)—use the Table Formatting Tools on the MODD Doc Tools toolbar to quickly apply the table text and table heading styles, along with the correct cell margins (all set to zero) and cell borders.

Apply the font and cell shading colors to match the design, using the Apply Design Color dialog box on the MODD Design And Layout toolbar.

This is a default formatted Word footnote (available from Insert, Reference, Footnote).

Note that the blue borders are paragraph borders that are part of the styles. Only the black borders in this table are cell borders.

That little flowchart is a very simple Word table—and an example of how to save time and get great results by using the simplest method available for the task.
Let's take a detailed look at how that flowchart is constructed:

1. If you start with the top two rows of the layout as mentioned in the previous diagram, make sure the bottom part of the layout has been split off first (Table, Split Table). Deselect Specify Height (Table, Table Properties, Row) for the second row and then select Table, Split Cells to split the single cell on the second row into seven columns and five rows.

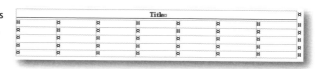

If you start by creating your own 7-column, 6-row table (Table, Insert, Table), just merge the cells of the top row and apply Table Group Heading style.

2. Merge the subheading cells and the first row heading, as you see here.

Then, just type the text and apply the styles as shown at right.

Timeline of Upcoming Releases							
	Q4 '04			Q1 '05			
	October	November	December	January	February	March	
Marketing Focus	(start Q3 '04)						
Release Date		Square Without Corners (11-10)		Backward to Tomorrow (1-16)		Night Bloomer (3-5)	

Paragraph styles used:

- Table Group Heading
- Table Heading
- Table Row Heading
- Table Text

Note: The non-printing character you see between the title and the date here is a line break. It starts a new line without starting a new paragraph. Press Shift+Enter at the end of a line to insert a line break.

3. The difference between the second and third tables here is nothing more than a bit of a color! (These specific colors are part of the active MODD Design.)

The green, orange and aqua font color, cell shading and cell borders can all be applied from the Apply Design Color dialog box on the MODD Design And Layout toolbar. Or, if you prefer to apply them yourself from Word's Font dialog box and Borders And Shading dialog box, see the MODD Design Color Guide at the back of this book for the correct RGB color settings.

Timeline of Upcoming Releases					
Q4 '04			Q1 '05		
October	November	December	January	February	March
Marketing Focus	(start Q3 '04)				
Release Date	Square Without Corners (11-10)		Backward to Tomorrow (1-16)		Night Bloomer (3-5)

You can use the same principles shown in the flowchart diagram to create that Word table on the bottom half of the page. Either create your own four-column, nine-row table (Table, Insert, Table) or start with the bottom two rows of the MODD Layout *2-Part Page, Top & Bottom*. To use the last two rows of the layout—once the layout has been split (Table, Split Table):

1. Click into the bottom row and deselect the Specify height setting through Table, Table Properties, Row.

2. Then, with your insertion point still in the bottom row, go to Table, Split Cells and split that single-cell row into four columns and eight rows.

Making Choices

As Voltaire was kind enough to point out at the beginning of this chapter, don't feel the need to put everything you're thinking on the page! The more text you give your readers, the less likely they are to read it all. Instead of leaving it to your reader to pick and choose what's important (and possibly miss the most essential points), make those choices yourself. No software can make your content accessible when the content itself isn't clear and directed. Providing sources for your facts supports your credibility, but if more information than that is warranted to back up a point, provide an appendix with your document. Emphasize the content you really need them to see—better to have them ask for more than to miss what you were saying in the first place.

On the same note, keep in mind that most of your readers don't have Superman's power of sight! If you have to reduce the font substantially to make it fit, split up the information instead. I can't tell you how many presentations I've seen that literally needed a magnifying glass to be read! Many companies' standards allow text on a presentation page to be as small as 4 or 5 points. Fonts that small might be fine for the occasional label on a graph where the reader is likely to understand the information without reading all the text labels, but using tiny font sizes on text you want your reader to pay attention to is another story.

Curious about what 4 point text looks like? I would have provided an image of it for you here, but you wouldn't be able to read it! Instead, open the file *4 Point Text Sample.doc* from your *MODD Samples* folder.

So what else is there to building great text pages? No doubt you can think of a thing or two you would like to do that can't be done with the tools we've discussed so far. Well, that's only half true—the key to getting nearly any formatting you might need can be found just by taking Word tables one step farther.

Nesting Tables

A nested table is nothing more than one table placed inside another. Doing this enables you to use the outside table (called the *host* table) as the page layout, and the inside table (the nested table) for content. In that way, you can place tables side by side and organize your content into easily digestible bites.

> **See Also:** Nesting tables can be a simple task, but there are rules to follow if you want them to be easy to build and to manage. If you aren't a nested table guru just yet, check out the article on nested tables, "Never Leave the Nest! Nesting Tables Is the Simple Solution to Amazing Documents," that was referenced at the start of this chapter.

The three diagrammed pages to follow provide detailed examples of great presentation pages that make use of nested tables, and offer tips for building these pages in little more time than it takes to read them.

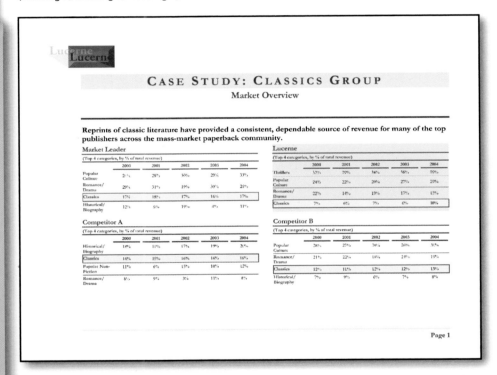

This document is a MODD Presentation/Report document in landscape orientation. As with the previous document, the header and footer are automatically created when the document is generated, along with the first presentation page containing the top three paragraph styles used on this page (Heading 1, Heading 2, Heading 3).

To create the nested tables shown here, start with the 4-Part Page MODD layout. When you insert it, it will automatically take on the active design (Moss Green in the case of the sample document).

1. With your insertion point in the cell labeled A (above), create a 6-column, 6-row table (Table, Insert, Table). You've just created a nested table!

2. Use the Table formatting tools on the MODD Doc Tools toolbar to automatically apply your table heading and table text styles, remove cell margins, and apply the black cell borders. Use the Apply Design Color dialog box to apply the coordinating shading and border colors for the highlighted row.

3. Once you've typed the text and are happy with the nested table's formatting—select the nested table (Table, Select, Table) and copy it just as you would text. Then, click in each of the other quadrants and paste and just edit each additional table as needed.

Tip: On this and any layouts that you use as a host table, you might want to deselect the Specify Height option in Table, Table Properties, Row for the rows where you're placing the nested tables, if you want those rows to adjust to the height of the nested tables rather than maintaining their own minimum height setting.

When you create nested tables, you don't need to use every cell of the table for nesting. In the previous sample page, as in this one, the headings for each nested quadrant are in their own cells of the host table (i.e., the layout).

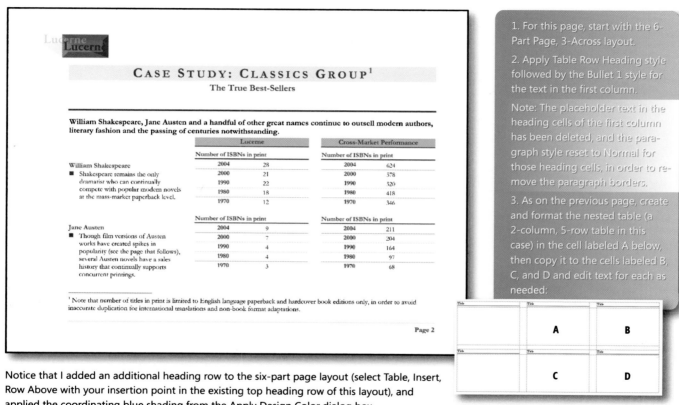

1. For this page, start with the 6-Part Page, 3-Across layout.

2. Apply Table Row Heading style followed by the Bullet 1 style for the text in the first column.

Note: The placeholder text in the heading cells of the first column has been deleted, and the paragraph style reset to Normal for those heading cells, in order to remove the paragraph borders.

3. As on the previous page, create and format the nested table (a 2-column, 5-row table in this case) in the cell labeled A below, then copy it to the cells labeled B, C, and D and edit text for each as needed:

Notice that I added an additional heading row to the six-part page layout (select Table, Insert, Row Above with your insertion point in the existing top heading row of this layout), and applied the coordinating blue shading from the Apply Design Color dialog box.

Can you figure out the correct dimensions and formatting for those four little nested tables in the bottom of this layout? Use the same method described on the preceding sample pages to recreate the nested tables on this page.

This page uses the 6-Part Page, 3-Down layout.

1. With your insertion point in the third row of the layout (the first small divider row that has the Between Rows paragraph style applied), select Table, Split Table. This will split off the first two rows of the layout. In the new paragraph between the split tables, apply Heading 3 style to type the text and insert the footnote you see here.

2. Apply Table Heading style to the first and third cells in that same divider row (containing the text Classic and Contemporary, respectively) and then apply the coordinating blue shading for those cells from the Apply Design Color dialog box, just as on the previous page.

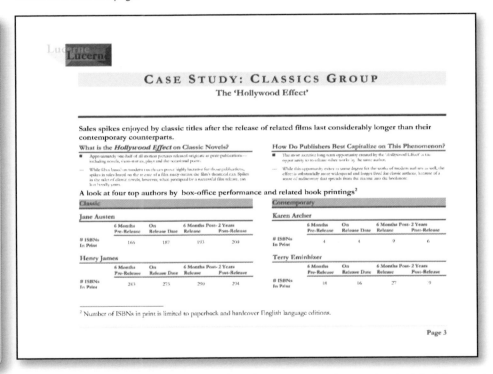

Tip: Once you create your own version of this document, open the completed original document (*Lucerne–Case Study.doc*, located in your *MODD Samples* folder) and compare it to yours to see how you did. Or, examine the completed original for help figuring out any details you aren't certain of, like the number of rows or columns in the tables and the paragraph formatting used.

Want a Way to Get It Done Even Faster?

Once you know how to nest one table inside another, take advantage of the tables you already have at your disposal. Remember that most MODD layouts are tables, and can be nested inside one another. For best results, start with one of the layouts that's designed to be a host table and nest other layouts inside of it for unique, creative, and beautiful pages.

Check out the two diagrammed pages that follow. These pages nest some of the pre-created layouts for quick and simple documents that look anything but quick and simple.

Notice the use of white space on these diagrammed pages. Tables help you provide balance and leave white space for clean-looking layouts regardless of your document's design. Avoiding the urge to fill in that white space—particularly when you use a bold design such as in the last two sample diagrams shown here—can help keep bright colors and chunky fonts from becoming overwhelming.

Note Keep in mind that the MODD layouts and designs are provided as examples—jumping off points to customize and build on as you like. Use them as they are or create and save your own. If you've never before thought of Microsoft Office as a creative set of tools, isn't it a lot more fun this way?

Note: When you nest one MODD layout inside another, you'll get a paragraph mark above the nested table that you may not want. Just click into that paragraph and delete it...

This sample document uses the Smashing Purple MODD design.

The layout used for the host table is the 2-Columns (for nested tables) layout.

1. With your insertion point in the first column of the table, insert the 1-Object Page layout (it will insert as a nested table).

2. With your insertion point in the third column (notice that there is a second, middle column in the host table that's used as a divider) insert the 2-Part Page, Top & Bottom layout as a nested table.

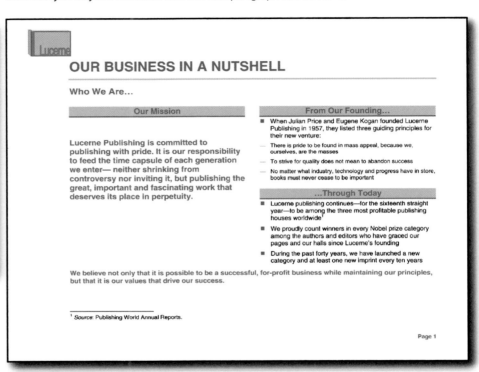

...the reason MODD does this is that when you try to insert one table inside another—especially into the first column of the host table—Word may attach the tables instead of nesting them. Placing a space or a paragraph in the host cell before nesting the table causes Word to see what you're trying to do, and you can just delete any unwanted space after your table is nested.

This page starts with the 3-Columns (for nested tables) layout.

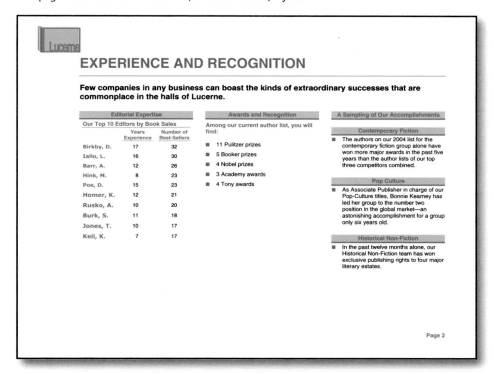

1. I added a second row to the layout (Table, Insert, Rows Above) in order to use the top row of the host table as the headings (Table Group Heading style is applied to the cells of that row, except in the divider columns).

2. Insert your own nested table into the first column of the layout, and format using the appropriate table heading and table text styles (the nested table is 12-rows by 3-columns).

3. The center of this layout has a paragraph with Table Row Heading style applied followed by bullets (Bullet 1 style), all directly in the host cell.

4. In the last column, I inserted a 2-Part Page, Top & Bottom layout, then copied the bottom three rows (starting with the divider row) and pasted them directly below this nested table to add them to the bottom of that table. Now, I have a nested table in 3 parts from top-to-bottom.

Tip: When you paste rows of a table directly below an existing table, Word connects the new rows as part of the existing table. If you want to paste rows below a table as their own, separate table, just press Enter to place a paragraph mark between the old and new tables. Notice that when you split tables in this chapter's previous samples (using Table, Split Table), Word splits the tables by placing a paragraph mark between them.

Next Steps and Quick Reference

Now that you're ready to make quick work of your complex text pages, the chapter to follow will introduce you to some key features that Excel has to offer your documents. But first, here's a quick overview of the MODD designs and layouts used in the samples throughout this chapter:

MODD Designs Used in This Chapter

TRIED AND TRUE NAVY BLUE

CLASSIC MOSS GREEN

SMASHING PURPLE

Layouts Used in This Chapter:
The MODD Page Organizing Layouts

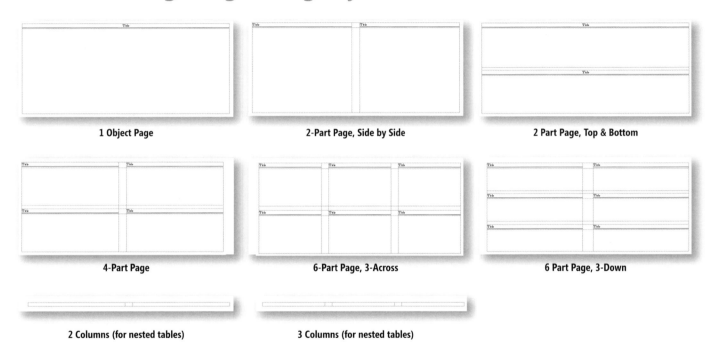

1 Object Page

2-Part Page, Side by Side

2 Part Page, Top & Bottom

4-Part Page

6-Part Page, 3-Across

6 Part Page, 3-Down

2 Columns (for nested tables)

3 Columns (for nested tables)

04

Putting a Face on Your Facts:
Using Excel charts for high-impact documents

Take a look at some of the important documents you've created in the past. How much filler surrounds your facts? Come on, we all do it! Look at the documents you receive—how much of the detail that the writers couldn't do without could you gladly do without and still understand what they wanted to say?

So, consider how much stronger some of your points might be made if you were able to replace paragraphs, a table (even a page!) with a single, powerful image. That's where we turn to Excel.

1. *Make your point visually* **2.** *Let Excel find the Spin* **3.** *Approach charting efficiently* **4.** *Get creative with Excel* **5.** *Show off your chart's best side*

"Fillet the fish. Throw the rest away." —Kurt Vonnegut

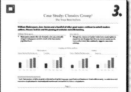

How Do I... Articles and Tip Sheets to Help With the Tasks in This Chapter

Topic	Article of Tip Sheet Title
Excel basics	"Making Your Excel Workbooks Behave!"
	"What Happened to My...? Common Errors, Their Causes and How to Avoid Them"
Selecting chart types and understanding chart basics	"Chart Anatomy 101: Understanding Chart Elements and Selecting the Best Chart for Your Data"
Creating a chart	New to the Feature: "Columns and Bars and Pies, Oh My! Creating a Basic Excel Chart"
	More Experienced: "Editing Charts and Using Chart Options" or "Advanced Chart Types: 3-D, Multi-Axis, Combinations, Scatters, and Bubbles"
Using drawing objects in charts	"Fighter-Pilot Cool: Charting Tips, Tricks, and Troubleshooting"
Sizing Excel charts for Word	"Simple Sizing in a Snap! Sizing Excel Charts for Word Documents on the First Try"
Place Excel charts in Word	"Getting Your Excel, PowerPoint, or Any Graphic Into Word"
Creating PivotTables	"Your Very Own Spin Doctor! Creating PivotTables and Charts Is Easier Than You Think!"

In this chapter, we will take another approach to the documents from Chapter 03. We'll look at where we can incorporate Excel charts to slim down and punch up those pages, as well as how to let Excel show you the most effective way for presenting your particular data.

Though we'll be looking at the same documents here as in the previous chapter, you'll notice that they use three new design approaches. If you're trying these projects for yourself, save time and unnecessary typing by starting with the documents you created in Chapter 03. Just make a copy of the document (to retain your original) and apply the new design (from Apply Design, MODD Design on the MODD Design And Layout toolbar in Word). All elements of your document formatted with paragraph styles that were part of the design (such as the page headings, table headings and text, bullets, etc.) will automatically change to match the newly applied design.

Note After you apply a new design to a MODD document, any elements you formatted using the Apply Design Color dialog box in Word (on the MODD Design And Layout toolbar) will not automatically re-color. Your new design's colors will be automatically available in that dialog box, however, for quick access and easy editing.

A Picture Is Worth at Least a Few Hundred Words

Let's look again at that chart page from the beginning of Chapter 03. (Yup, the page you see on the next page is exactly the same, except that it uses the *Academic Gold* MODD Design.)

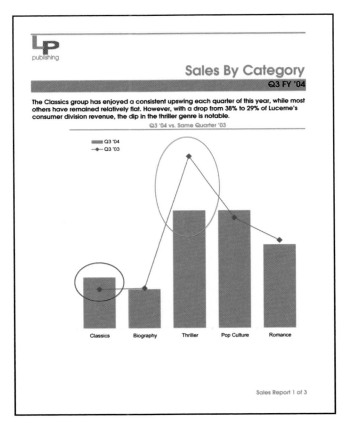

This page has two points to make and makes them clearly: it shows a continued revenue climb for one category (Classics) and a distinct drop for another (Thrillers). The ovals that overlay key items on the chart are what compel you to read the accompanying text. And that single paragraph of text is all that's needed to explain those two points—including providing specific figures where necessary. Clean, simple, strong.

Want to create this page for yourself? Take a look at how it's built:

Find this completed document in your MODD Samples folder, named *Lucerne - Sales Charted.doc*.

Note: Always create charts on their own sheet, for ease of sizing and formatting.

Note: Always size a chart before adding outside elements like the oval AutoShapes

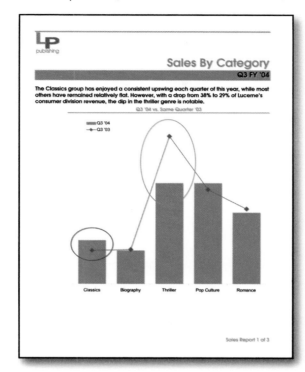

To create this chart, use the data you'll find in Lucerne Data – Sales 04.xls. (Note that the completed chart is also there if you want to compare it to your own!)

1. Create a clustered column chart. (This is the default sub-type when you select Column as your chart type in the Chart Wizard).

2. Use MODD's Chart Design Colors tool to recolor this chart to match the design of the Word document.

3. Select the Q4 '03 series and then select Line With Markers from the Chart Type dialog box (Chart, Chart Type).

4. Size the chart to fit that 1-Object Page layout used on the Word page. (I used the Size My Chart button on the MODD Excel Design Tools toolbar to do that instantly.)

5. Add the ovals from the Drawing toolbar in Excel. When you use the Line Color icon on the drawing toolbar to recolor them, you'll see that your design's colors (Academic Gold, in this case) are also available here—as the last two lines in the color palette.

As you know from the previous chapter, this is a MODD Presentation/Report document. The logo, heading styles and footer were added automatically when I created the document.

In fact, to start this document, you can just make a copy of *Lucerne – Sales Report.doc* and then apply this new design (Academic Gold) from Apply Design, MODD Design on the MODD Design And Layout toolbar.

Of course, before you can build Excel charts that make your points for you, you need to start by knowing what chart type is best for the particular data! With the chart on this page, for example, you might try a clustered column chart, like so:

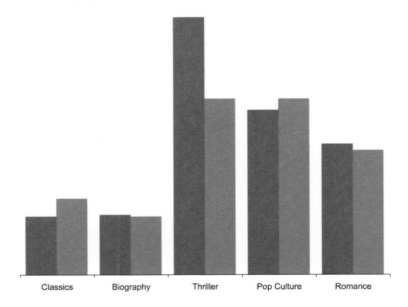

In fact, as you saw in the preceding diagram of this sample page, clustered columns are the best way to start the chart that we ended up with.

Notice that the difference in height of the side-by-side columns for the Classics category doesn't make much of a statement. Well, if you wanted to stick with this chart type, you could alter the minimum and maximum values used to chart your data (the y-axis scale)—the smaller the scale, the larger slight differences will appear to be. Remember, the chart Excel gives you to start with has a lot of possibilities. You can customize any chart element you need to get your point across. So, let's take a closer look at this example of altering the scale:

Since we deleted the y-axis from this chart, we'll first need to bring it back (just temporarily) in order to change its scale, as follows:

1. Go to Chart, Chart Options, Axes, click to select Value (Y) Axis, and click OK. The y-axis will reappear.

2. Double-click on the y-axis to open the Format Axis dialog box. On the Scale tab, change the values for Minimum and Maximum as desired.

    For example, the existing minimum value for this chart is 0 and the existing maximum is 180. Changing these values to 20 and 160, respectively, will still accommodate all of your data but tightens the scale to make differences between values appear more significant.

3. After you close out of that dialog box, if you're happy with the new scale you can simply click to select the y-axis and then press Delete on your keyboard to remove the axis from view.

If you tried that for yourself, you see that making that change does help to make the point, but I wanted a more cut-and-dried solution for such a big, bold image. Using the combination chart type in this case helped to distinguish more clearly between the two data series. And, looking beyond this simple chart, check out the next section of this chapter to see how different chart types can make *entirely different* statements about your data.

Determining the Best Way to Display Your Data

Take a look at one charted example of a page primarily created with tables in the previous chapter:

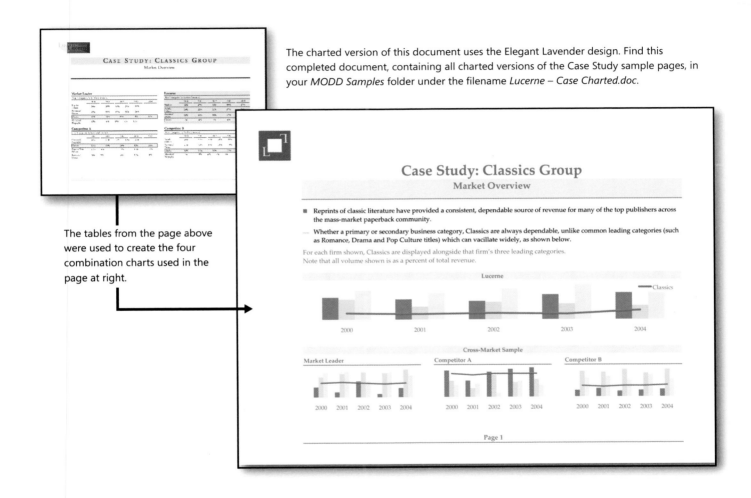

The charted version of this document uses the Elegant Lavender design. Find this completed document, containing all charted versions of the Case Study sample pages, in your *MODD Samples* folder under the filename *Lucerne – Case Charted.doc*.

The tables from the page above were used to create the four combination charts used in the page at right.

The charted version you see in the preceding diagram is certainly a nice-looking page. Our company (Lucerne) is emphasized over the competition, and we can clearly see the primary point of the page in the consistent, deep purple line series that appears in each chart. Sure, these charts show the stated point that the Classics category is a consistent and dependable source of revenue, more consistent in fact than several larger categories. Notice, however, that the purpose of the page is to show how Classics is a smart source of revenue, yet our charts also show that our company has a lower percentage of revenue in that category than any competitor! A strong statement, perhaps—but not the one you want to make to your boss, client, or anyone receiving this document!

The numbers in the tables from the text version of this page were all percentages of total revenue and, as you know, pie charts are a great way to show contributions to a total. Also, since the purpose of this page is not to set us apart from our competitors, combining our numbers with those of our competitors makes a more positive, cleaner statement. Here is the version of this page that I'd prefer to send to a client:

This page started with the 4-Part 1/2 Page layout, then added another divider column and another content column to accommodate the fifth chart.

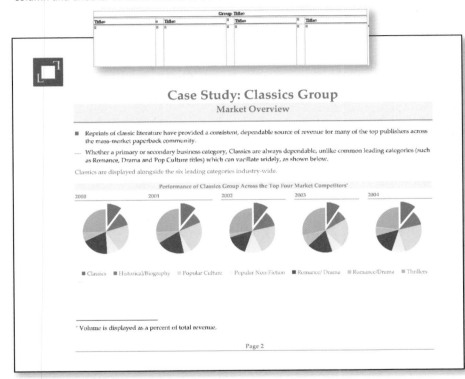

To create the pies:

1. Create one pie on its own sheet.

2. Apply the Elegant Lavender design.

3. Format and size the chart to fit the Word table.

4. Explode the appropriate slice of the pie.

Do all of this before copying the first chart to make the others! That way, all you'll have to do is copy that chart sheet four times and change the data for each. Excel will make all necessary adjustments for your new data!

How did I get one legend to share for all five charts? (Actually, this legend is a chart!)

1. Copy the chart one extra time after the pies are formatted.

2. Create a single-cell table in Word that fits the shape you want for the legend, and then resize the last copy of the Excel chart to fit your single-cell table.

3. Chart legends have white fill by default and will hide the plot area of the chart when the two overlap.

So, just ignore the pie and drag the legend to take up the entire space of the newly sized chart.

4. Then, copy the 'chart' into the single-cell Word table just as you to the pie charts (use MODD's Copy Chart To Word tool to do this for you instantly and perfectly every time).

I used a PivotTable to help determine the best way to show this data, as well as to do the calculating for me. PivotTables have a scary reputation, but it's totally undeserved! Not only can they be simple to create, but they are awesome tools for analyzing your data in a fraction of the time that it would take using any other method! PivotTables help you to quickly see your data from various angles just by dragging and dropping your data fields from one part of the chart to another! See the article "Your Very Own Spin Doctor! Creating PivotTables and Charts Is Easier Than You Think!" for step-by-step instructions on creating and working with basic PivotTables, and check out the table I used to crunch the numbers of this pie chart page in the file Lucerne Data - Case 04.xls, located in your MODD Samples folder.

However, once you decide on the type of chart you need, you might want to copy data from your PivotTable to another sheet before creating your charts, as I did for the pie chart sample page. When you create a chart from a PivotTable (called a PivotChart), you do get the benefit of being able to swap what data is shown in the chart as easily as the drag-and-drop method used to alter the PivotTable. There are also limitations to PivotCharts, however, including that you'll lose most custom formatting when you change which data is visible and, though you can choose to hide fields on the PivotChart, you can't create a chart from just part of a PivotTable's data. The referenced article will give you more information on PivotCharts as well, and you can find an example of a finished PivotChart in the same sample file (Lucerne Data – Case 04.xls) mentioned above.

Of course, most data is more straightforward about what type of chart is best. Take a look at the other two pages from our Case Study document, for smart and simple examples:

Note Remember that the data for these charts started off as 4 separate tables in the text version of this page. These charts are created by averaging those four sets of data to create one set of data per year. If you want to create these charts from scratch yourself, copy and paste the table data from *Lucerne-Case Study.doc* into an Excel workbook. Or, find the numbers already crunched for you on the Chart Data worksheet of the file *Lucerne Data – Case 04.xls*.

The four column charts on this page correspond directly to the four nested tables that appear on the text version of this page from Chapter 03.

Just like the pie charts on the preceding sample page, format and size the first column chart you create before copying it to create the other three—you'll save tons of time and get much better results.

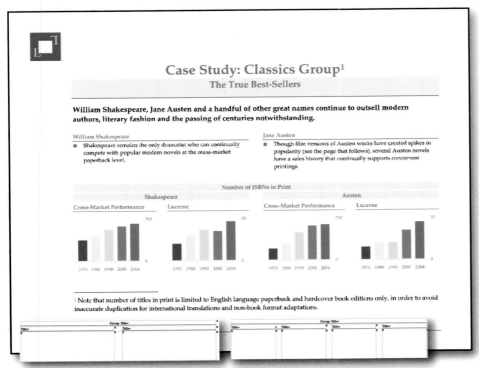

For a Y-Axis that shows only the top and bottom numbers as you see in the column charts here:

1. Double-click on the Y-Axis to get to the Format Axis dialog box and select the Scale tab.

3. If the Minimum Value is set to zero, just change the Major Unit value to match the Maximum Value.

Note: If you're creating a chart with a minimum value other than zero, get this same effect by subtracting the Minimum value from the Maximum value and using the result of that calculation as your Major Unit.

This page starts with the 2 Part 1/2 Page layout on top and the 4 Part 1/2 Page layout on the bottom. As you see, I deleted the top row of the 2 part layout and added an extra heading row to the bottom.

Note that the data labels are shown on these charts instead of the Y-Axis. In fact, none of the sample chart pages you'll see here use both a Y-Axis and data labels. That's because using both is overkill! Just as in the text of your document, the cleaner you keep your charts—the more powerful a statement they make. Decide which (if either) way of showing the specific values associated with a chart is best for expressing that chart's particular purpose.

Tip: If your x-axis labels insist on slanting, they're just trying to help you make room! Even so, there is an easy fix:

1. Double-click the axis to open the Format Axis dialog box, then click the Alignment tab.

2. Deselect the zero that appears in the box labeled Degrees and re-type the zero. This turns off the Automatic option you'll see selected at the top of the dialog box.

3. When you click OK to close the dialog box, your labels will listen to you—even if there isn't room for them all! If they overlap, reduce the font size.

Since these charts are quite small and the x-axis labels need to be readable, split all x-axis labels onto 2-lines, as you see here—that will help you maximize font size.

To do this, just click into the cell for each axis label (in the source data) and press Alt+Enter before the word you want to wrap to the second line.

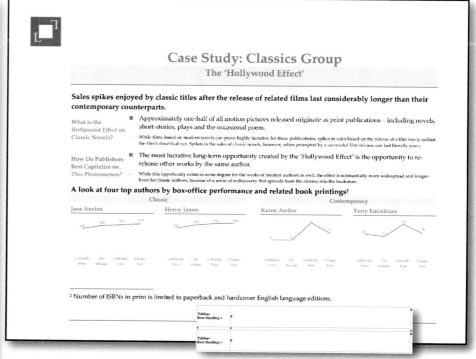

The bulleted text on this page with headings beside it used the 2-Part 1/2 Page, Left Title layout shown here. The four part table on the bottom of the page uses the same layout as the bottom of the previous diagrammed page.

Notice that you can save yourself a minute on customizing the headings of this page's four-part layout by copying the already-edited four-part layout from the previous page and just deleting the top row.

Note Notice that several of the sample pages in this chapter are substantially reorganized from their text versions in Chapter 03—even though they contain most of the same information. The primary reason is that charts, as you've seen, can help you crystallize the point of the page. When you extrapolate which data has strong enough legs to make a statement for you, the resulting chart can put an entirely different—and more persuasive—spin on the page than you originally intended.

So, we've seen how important it is to know everything your chart might be saying, as well as how very simple charts can make very powerful communicators. Now, how about content that has numbers attached but not necessarily numbers that make for easy (or any) charting? Well, whoever said that you can't fit a square peg in a round hole should have tried making the circle a little wider!

Coloring Outside of Excel's Lines

Sometimes breaking the rules just opens up more possibilities. Take the sample page that follows, for example. The timeline you'll see on the right half of the page is just an Excel scatter chart, born from one of the bullets on the text version of this page: "During the past 40 years, we have launched a new category and at least one new imprint every 10 years."

By showing the timeline in place of that bullet, you not only honor the favorite writing-school maxim of "show, don't tell"—you get to make the point about the firm's rapid growth while at the same time displaying each individual success visually (in this case, listing the names of all of the firm's book categories and publishing imprints). It makes an appealing centerpiece for the page, makes the firm's growth look impressive, and still leaves ample room for the other information we want to include. Of course, the fact that there's no data for Excel to plot might seem like a *teensy* wrinkle in our plan, but it's no problem at all in this case! Just follow the instructions in the diagram that follows to try it yourself, or check out the completed chart in the file *Lucerne Data - Overview 04.xls*, located in your *MODD Samples* folder.

This page uses the 1-Part 1/2 Page, Left Title layout on top and the 3-Part 1/2 Page, Wide Right layout on the bottom. Notice that, though they're called half-page layouts, you can adjust the row height to take up whatever portion of the page you need for each.

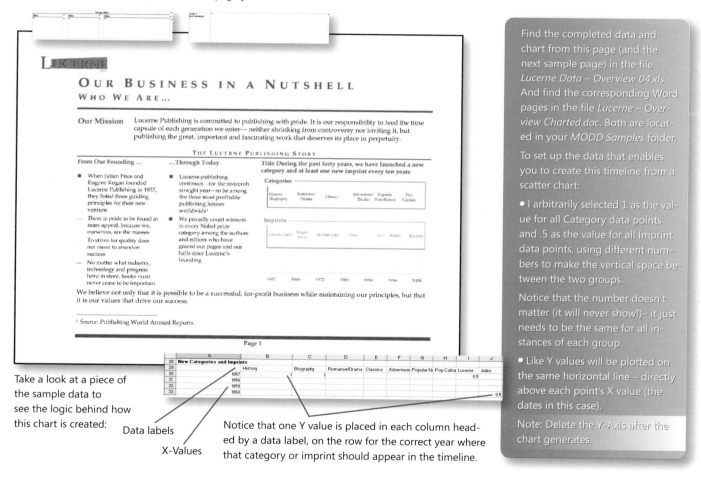

Take a look at a piece of the sample data to see the logic behind how this chart is created:

Data labels

X-Values

Notice that one Y value is placed in each column headed by a data label, on the row for the correct year where that category or imprint should appear in the timeline.

Find the completed data and chart from this page (and the next sample page) in the file *Lucerne Data – Overview 04.xls*. And find the corresponding Word pages in the file *Lucerne – Overview Charted.doc*. Both are located in your *MODD Samples* folder.

To set up the data that enables you to create this timeline from a scatter chart:

• I arbitrarily selected 1 as the value for all Category data points and .5 as the value for all Imprint data points, using different numbers to make the vertical space between the two groups.

Notice that the number doesn't matter (it will never show!)– it just needs to be the same for all instances of each group.

• Like Y values will be plotted on the same horizontal line – directly above each point's X value (the dates in this case).

Note: Delete the Y-Axis after the chart generates.

Here are a few more tips to help you with this timeline:

- When this timeline is generated from a scatter chart, each data point will have a marker in addition to the data label. Just set the markers to None (do this for each series through Format, Data Series, Patterns) so that all you see is the data label for each.

- Notice that the vertical lines in this timeline are just the chart's own gridlines (major and minor gridlines are used here).

- The Categories and Imprints text boxes, along with the rectangles that surround each group, can be created and recolored right from Excel's Drawing toolbar. (Remember that you'll avoid extra work by sizing the chart *before* adding these drawing elements!)

- For instructions that will help you quickly and easily get the *exact* start and end years for your x-axis, see the tip sheet "Fighter-Pilot Cool: Charting Tips, Tricks, and Troubleshooting."

Another example of coloring outside of Excel's lines was the legend shared by five pie charts on the first diagrammed page in this chapter. Like the timeline example, creating an extra chart that displays nothing but the legend is just taking full advantage of what's already at your fingertips—making the available tools work for you! For more ideas of how to stretch the possibilities with Excel charts, see the see the tip sheet referenced in the last bullet point above.

Okay, so you have the right chart. If you've got it, be sure you know how to flaunt it!

Showing Off Your Chart's Best Side

Let's take a look at charting one more sample page. In the sample page below, I chose to chart the Editorial Expertise table from the text version of this page shown in Chapter 03, and add a chart for the bullet from that version that read "As Associate Publisher in charge of our Pop Culture titles, Bonnie Kearney has led her group to the number two position in the global market—an astonishing accomplishment for a group only six years old."

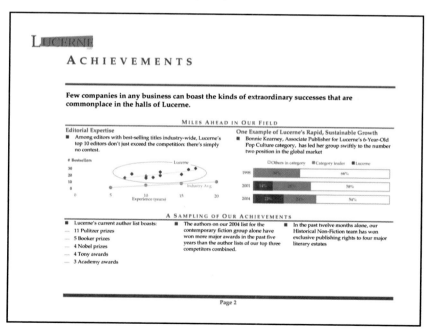

I added some comparative industry data to add muscle to the Editorial Expertise chart. And the Pop Culture category's growth chart adds concrete data to back up and emphasize an already impressive point. However, these charts aren't working as hard as they could for my document! The page is just too crowded.

Not every chart has to be as large as the one on the first sample page in this chapter. When you're trying to make a dramatic point, however, it's tough to be dramatic using tiny fonts and squished graphics! Consider moving the bottom half of that page to its own page and giving the charts room to breathe. Now, take a look at this page and you can really see what these two charts have to say.

The thing that makes the data on this scatter chart look impressive is the vertical distance between Lucerne's editors and the industry average.

Notice how much stronger the statement is when you give this chart some height as opposed to how it looked on the more crowded version of this page.

To get the trendlines that run through each series of the scatter chart:

1. Right-click on any data point in the series and select Add Trendline.

2. In the Add Trendline dialog box that opens, just click OK to insert the default, which is the linear trendline you see here. Note that the trendlines draw attention and exaggerate the gap between Lucerne and the industry average.

Remember: Save lots of formatting stress on that scatter chart by sizing the chart before you add the text boxes for Lucerne and Industry Average and the oval around the Lucerne series!

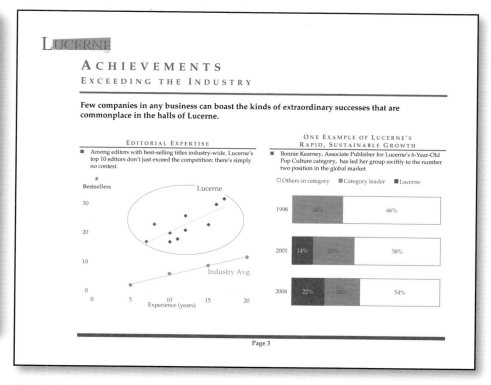

Though the data looks the same in both sizes of this bar chart—a bar chart's series are laid out vertically. So, notice how much stronger this chart looks when you give it a bit of height!

Next Steps and Quick Reference

Now that you can leap tall Excel charts in a single bound, check out the next chapter to learn how to use PowerPoint elements for organizing and illustrating your essential document content. That chapter will also show you a few tricks you might not expect from unassuming, mild-mannered PowerPoint—including a look at some of the logos you see throughout the sample documents in this *Design Guide* and even tips for breaking apart Clip Art to make your own, well—anything!

But first, check out the MODD Designs and Layouts demonstrated in this chapter.

MODD Designs Used in This Chapter

Academic Gold

Elegant Lavender

GRAND CRU BURGUNDY

Layouts Used in This Chapter (and a Few of Their Friends): The MODD Half-Page Organizing Layouts

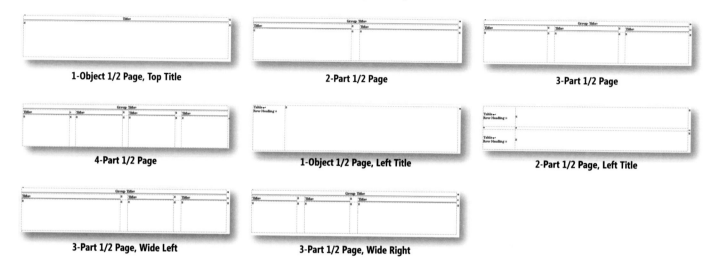

1-Object 1/2 Page, Top Title

2-Part 1/2 Page

3-Part 1/2 Page

4-Part 1/2 Page

1-Object 1/2 Page, Left Title

2-Part 1/2 Page, Left Title

3-Part 1/2 Page, Wide Left

3-Part 1/2 Page, Wide Right

We All Look at the Pictures!

Maximizing PowerPoint's potential in your Word documents

Think about your driver's license photo, your passport picture—or, maybe that impromptu 6 a.m. shot, the one before you'd brushed your hair or even counted the pillow creases on your cheek. Would you put it on your résumé? Your holiday party invitation? The announcement of your Academy Award nomination? Of course not! Because, good or bad, the picture *always* stands out.

That said, this chapter isn't just about adding PowerPoint pictures to your documents. You won't see cartoon people pointing at important paragraphs here (and please, don't do that!). We're going to look at using PowerPoint to add strength to your documents; to organize the points you want to make; and to get your readers to notice exactly what you want them to see.

1. *Use graphics for clarity* **2.** *Use graphics for organization* **3.** *Find the right graphics for the document* **4.** *Build complex diagrams easily* **5.** *Get creative with PowerPoint*

"I try to leave out the parts readers skip." —Elmore Leonard

How Do I... Articles and Tip Sheets to Help With the Tasks in This Chapter

Topic	Article or Tip Sheet Title
PowerPoint essentials	"Making Your PowerPoint Objects Behave"
Basics of creating PowerPoint graphics	"The Essentials of a Good Figure: Working With Shapes (Including Lines and Connectors)"
	"Creating and Editing Text Objects: Placeholders, Autoshapes, Custom Text Boxes, and WordArt"
	"The Draw Menu: Spacing, Alignment, and Distribution"
Fighter-pilot-cool PowerPoint graphics	"Creating Custom Objects With Edit Points"
	"Using Shadows, 3-D, and Fill Effects"
	"Advanced Picture Tools: Save Object as a Picture; Cropping, Recoloring, Etc."
	"Tips, Tricks, and Troubleshooting for PowerPoint Objects"

Once again, we're going to look at new ways to approach the three documents we created in Chapter 03. The samples in this chapter use three new design approaches to the Word documents, while adding some key PowerPoint graphics. And, now that you also have a feel for Word and Excel's potential in your documents, the samples we'll create here look at getting more adventurous with page layouts to bring the best elements of Word, Excel, and PowerPoint together in your document.

Sometimes Less Really Is More

The presentation graphics that fit your particular document might be intricate, but more often than not they're very simple. A clean, simple, even spare image can often convey more to your reader than a complex diagram or paragraphs of text. For example, take a look at the left-hand page in the image that follows, from the Lucerne Publishing sales report document we built in Chapter 03. In that chapter, we created the marketing timeline you see here using a Word table—which was a clear, readable solution for organizing that content. However, simplified further in a small PowerPoint flow chart, the page on the right of this image gets cleaner still— conveying the same information in a way that's even more accessible for the reader.

To set up the new page on the right, start with the MODD Full-Page layout Left Page Headings, Bulleted Text Page.

Then:

1. Delete the bullets on the right side of the layout and nest the Page Organizing layout 1-Object Page in that now empty large cell.

2. Adjust the height of the layout to leave space for your flowchart, but still accommodate the table beneath.

3. Then just press enter to add a paragraph return below the 1-Object Page layout and paste (nest) the table from the bottom half of the page.

Remember that adding that paragraph return between the two nested tables is an important step. Without a paragraph mark between any two tables, they become attached. And, since they're very different tables, that would cause unnecessary, unpleasant complications when it comes time to edit the page.

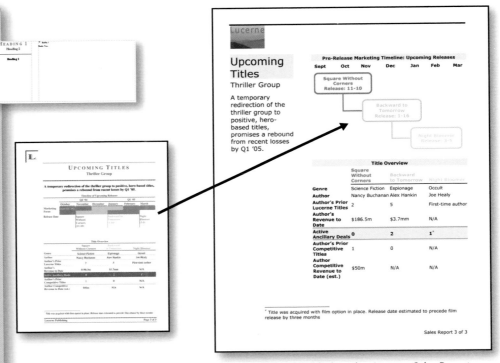

Explore the live version of the right-hand page above, along with the other Lucerne Sales Report pages reformatted in this design (and using MODD's Full-Page layouts), in the file *Lucerne – Sales Combined.doc*, located in your *MODD Samples* folder. The live PowerPoint diagram is in the same folder, in a file named *Lucerne Sales – Graphic.ppt*.

Important: Before you start creating any PowerPoint object for your Word document, save yourself a lot of editing time later by creating a sizing guide that shows you the size of the space reserved for the object in your Word document.

As long as you're using a sized table cell as a place-holder for your graphic, MODD can do this for you with just a couple of clicks:

1. Place your insertion point in Word in the place-holder table cell.

2. In PowerPoint, click Create Sizing Guide on the MODD PowerPoint Design Tools toolbar.

When you no longer need this sizing guide, click Clear Sizing Guide on the same toolbar to remove it.

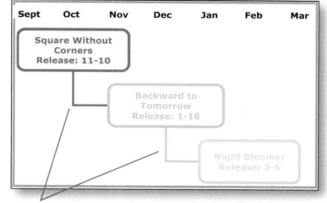

These lines that match the formatting of the rectangles are Connectors (available from the AutoShapes menu on the Drawing toolbar). Whenever possible, use Connectors for the lines in a flowchart or diagram, as they will automatically connect to the exact center or corner of an object's edge for simple, quick alignment—and they adjust themselves when attached objects move.

However, the vertical lines that reach from the months through the rectangles are actually drawn lines. That's because I needed more flexibility for where they start and end, relative to other objects in the diagram. If you aren't joining Connectors to an automatic connection point, drawing lines will give you more precision for ultimately less work.

Keep in mind that PowerPoint is all about efficiency. The more efficient you are, the more precise your results will be. For example:

1. Create and format one text box for Sept, then duplicate it for the other months and change the text, rather than creating and formatting seven separate text boxes.

2. Create one rounded rectangle, size it, apply the line, font and fill formatting before you duplicate it to create the two additional rounded rectangles. Then, you'll only have to change the color, text and adjust the width.

Notice that the width of these three rectangles each differs slightly. This is because the purpose of these rectangles is to demonstrate the span of time used for pre-release marketing of the film, and each is released (as you see in the diagram text) at a different point in the month.

Note: Quickly apply the line and font colors to match your Word document from the Apply Design Color dialog box on the MODD PowerPoint Design Tools toolbar.

3. Use the Align And Distribute options on the Drawing toolbar's Draw menu to top align and horizontally distribute the vertical lines, to vertically distribute the rectangles, and to top align the dates. The Align And Distribute tools are infinitely faster than nudging and much more precise.

That's a super-basic flow chart, but it also raises an essential point: if you're going to add graphic elements to your document—any graphic elements—make them *beautiful*. Crooked lines and misaligned or missized shapes draw the attention away from your information and instead make any number of statements that you certainly didn't intend. And the worst part about an image that's not created well? Working in PowerPoint, you can always bet that getting it perfect would have been faster and easier than getting it close.

How about using graphics to organize your document's content? Take a look at the little flow chart on the next page, for example.

Note You might be thinking that you'd use the Insert Diagram Or Organization Chart tool (available on the Drawing toolbar) to create a simple flow chart like the one we just looked at—but I encourage you to use AutoShapes and do this on your own. That diagram tool can come in handy (see the tip sheet "Tips, Tricks, and Troubleshooting for PowerPoint Objects" for ideas on how to make use of Office's diagram tool), but you get much more flexibility with little additional work when you use Power-Point's native tools to create objects—whether you need a simple diagram or a complex organization chart.

Explore the live version of these pages in the file *Lucerne – Case Combined.doc*, located in your *MODD Samples* folder. The live PowerPoint diagrams are in the same folder, in a file named *Lucerne Case – Graphic.ppt*.

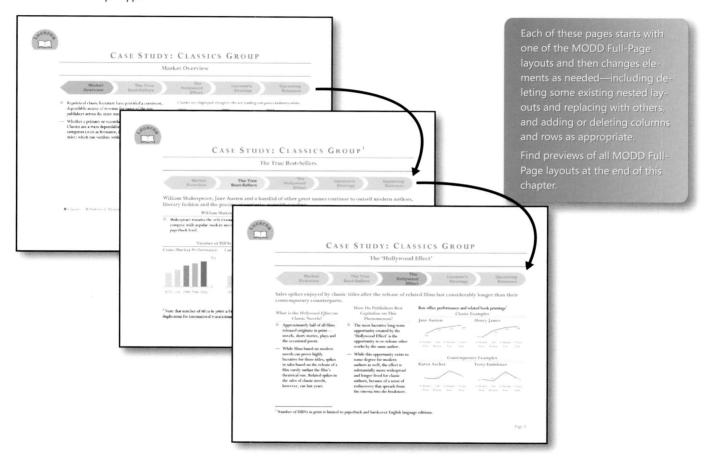

Each of these pages starts with one of the MODD Full-Page layouts and then changes elements as needed—including deleting some existing nested layouts and replacing with others, and adding or deleting columns and rows as appropriate.

Find previews of all MODD Full-Page layouts at the end of this chapter.

By just highlighting a different shape for each new page or new topic within the document, you give your readers a sense of progress as they turn the pages—reminding them of what they've already seen, highlighting the current point and letting them know what's still to come. And it took about five minutes total to create the versions of this flow chart for *all* pages.

Notice from the diagrams shown on the next page that more pages are intended for this case study document than we've created in our document sample. This type of flow chart provides the most benefit in longer documents, and can be especially useful when several pages of the document belong to the same topic—so that the highlighted element in the flow chart changes by topic rather than by page.

To create these flowchart diagrams, I used two shapes from the Flowchart group on the AutoShapes menu. Though flowchart shapes can represent specific types of data (those used here are named Display and Stored Data), you can surely use them in this type of diagram as well, just for shape options that are less frequently used.

Before starting to create this graphic:

1. I created a single-cell table in Word to the size of the intended graphic and copied it onto each page of the document to ensure that the graphic would fit.

2. Then, before deleting that single-cell table, I used it to add the red sizing guide you see here, using MODD's Create Sizing Guide tool mentioned earlier in this chapter.

Note: And remember, just as with Excel charts, you can use MODD's Copy Object to Word tool in PowerPoint to place your completed object in the document as an inline picture, along with a comment that provides the name and location of your PowerPoint file for future editing needs.

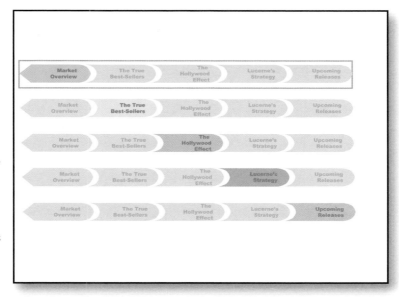

Tip: You can change text box margins as well as the vertical and horizontal Text Anchor Point (Format, AutoShape, Text Box) on any AutoShapes containing text to help your text fit well within whatever shape you choose.

To create this quickly, easily, and precisely:

1. Start by creating, then sizing and formatting just 1 of each type of shape.

2. Next, duplicate the shape with the concave end three more times and change the text as needed to complete the row.

3. Use the Align and Distribute tools to perfectly align the shapes vertically and distribute them horizontally.

4. Group the row of shapes, then duplicate it four times (use Ctrl+D to duplicate) to create the four additional single-row diagrams you see here. Then, just change the color of the appropriate shape on each successive row.

Go Ahead and Be Graphic!

If you're thinking you'd like to try something a bit more audacious than the basic diagrams we've looked at so far, you're going to enjoy this! When you need to say a lot with one flow chart, organization chart, or diagram, PowerPoint makes it easy to find creative ways to get your content noticed.

Remember this timeline we created using an Excel scatter chart in the preceding chapter?

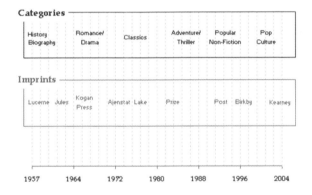

Using an Excel chart gave us the opportunity to express much more about an important, impressive fact than we originally had with simple bulleted text. But using PowerPoint for the same object lets us go one step bolder. Take a look at the Word page containing our timeline now.

That diagrammed timeline is nothing more than a handful of AutoShapes. Making use of our design's colors along with some fun formatting effects, we add dimension and impact to the same information shown in the Excel version. So, should we have used PowerPoint all along to create this timeline? Not necessarily. The decision should be based on who your reader is and what you want him to get from your timeline.

Find this completed page in the file *Lucerne – Overview Combined.doc*, located in your *MODD Samples* folder. The editable PowerPoint diagram (both versions you'll see in the diagrams that follow) can be found in the same folder, in a file named *Lucerne Overview – Graphic.ppt*.

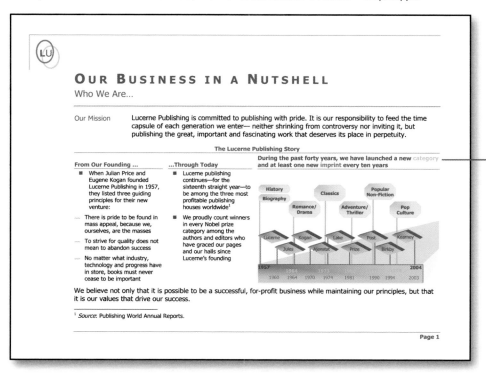

Notice that, to keep the graphic as clean as possible, I just changed the font color of the words category and imprint in the table heading to match the graphic, rather than adding a legend to the already complex diagram.

The Excel version looks like a data-driven chart. So, while it's graphic, it's understated and provides a sense that you're looking at data—that is, unadulterated fact. On the other hand, the PowerPoint version is eye-catching—it's bold, so it draws the reader in. While it contains the same factual information, the PowerPoint graphic is more about getting a sense of how much the firm has grown—as well as recognizing the firm's categories and imprints—than it is about conveying historical data.

Perhaps you're thinking about something in between? If you like the boldness of a PowerPoint graphic, but your style is somewhat softer than the timeline we just looked at, take a look at this:

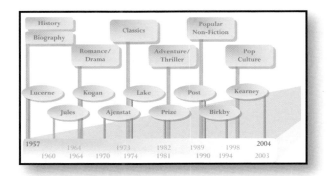

Note PowerPoint is definitely the best place to go for your presentation graphics—flow charts, accent graphics, most org charts, even logos (as we're about to see). But if you create a lot of complex diagrams such as network diagrams, floor plans, or other technical flow charts—particularly those related to content in other Microsoft Office applications, such as Excel or Project—you might want to think about adding Visio to your repertoire. Check out the Visio home page for information, demos, and downloads at office.microsoft.com/visio. At the time this book went to press, a free trial of Visio 2003 was available at this site for download; check the Microsoft site for details.

By changing colors and a few easy formatting options, we get a very different feel with very little work. The second version of that PowerPoint timeline uses MODD's Legacy Silver design. It took about two minutes to convert the first version to the second. Let's take a look at how both were created:

For the fills on the octagons, diamonds, and timeline rectangle, I started by applying my document's design colors from the MODD Apply Design Colors tool. Then I added a Gradient effect from the Fill Effects dialog box, available from the Fill Color pop-up menu on the Drawing toolbar.

Note that the vertical lines here are lines rather than connectors, because I wanted the flexibility to have the lines intersect the shapes wherever appropriate on the timeline.

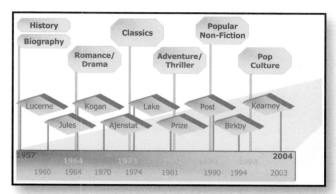

Tip: The 3-D effect on the diamonds is customized. You can customize the depth, perspective, lighting, surface, even color of the 3-D formatting by clicking 3-D Settings on the 3-D Style pop-up menu at the end of the Drawing toolbar.

The gray 3-D object behind the timeline adds a nice sense of movement and dimension (no pun intended) to our timeline.

In order to have it fall behind the diamonds and lines, it can't be 3-D formatting on the red rectangle itself. So, I duplicated the rectangle and applied the 3-D style to the new one, so that I could place it behind the other objects.

Since the new object's face is the same size as the red rectangle, all you see is the 3-D formatting, just as if it was part of the red rectangle itself.

Also, as the original PowerPoint 3-D formatting continues far to the right in order to provide this angle, I cut the 3-D shape and pasted it back as a picture, then cropped the picture from the right for the 3-D shape you see here.

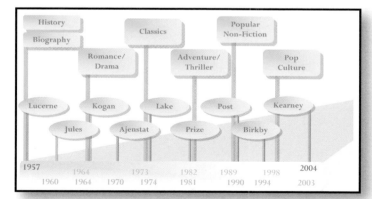

The dates are best placed as separate text boxes on top of the Timeline rectangle rather than trying to type them all in one text box – in order to make it easier to place and align them.

Going from the above diagram to this one took almost no time at all!

1. I applied the new design's colors using the Apply Design Colors tool and the gradient fill adjusted automatically to take on the new colors.

2. Next, I selected the group of Octagons (as well as the timeline rectangle) and used Change AutoShape on the Draw menu to change them to rounded rectangles. Then, I removed the 3-D effect from the diamonds and used Change AutoShape to change the diamonds to ovals.

3. I applied shadows to the rounded rectangles, ovals and vertical lines and used Shadow Settings (available from the Shadow Style pop-up menu on the Drawing toolbar) to move the shadows closer to the objects.

103

Pushing the Envelope and Having Fun Doing It!

Wondering if PowerPoint can get more creative than applying 3-D or shadow formatting to an AutoShape? Wonder no more! Edit pictures, break apart Clip Art to create your own shapes, use WordArt for seriously artistic text, and use Edit Points to create shapes you've never even considered. To demonstrate how fast and easy this can be—and the kind of results you can expect here with little work and even a bit of fun—let's look at how some of the more interesting Lucerne logos used in these project chapters were created.

Note To examine the live PowerPoint versions of the logos shown here, and all Lucerne logos used in this *Design Guide*, open the file *Lucerne Logos.ppt* from your *MODD Samples* folder.

If you don't recognize a couple of the logos demonstrated here, it's because they're still to come in the documents we'll create in Chapter 06.

While you're looking at these logos, keep in mind that, once you've finished creating a logo in PowerPoint (or any object that you'll need to save in its own picture file), you can right-click on the object and select Save as Picture. This will open the Save As Picture dialog box, where you can select a location, file name, and picture file type for your picture.

Notice that, for most objects, PowerPoint will default to the best picture type. Objects containing Office drawing shapes (i.e., AutoShapes, text boxes, etc.) will default to the Enhanced Windows Metafile picture type, which usually provides the best quality and file size for such objects.

While the remaining logos we'll see use a variety of other very cool features, this logo demonstrates that you might in fact not need more than a couple of AutoShapes and some simple formatting effects for a very professional logo.

To create this logo:

1. Insert the Bevel AutoShape (available from AutoShapes, Basic Shapes).

2. Use the adjustment handle (the yellow diamond) on the AutoShape to give it the jewel shape you see in the logo.

3. Use the Apply Design Colors dialog box on the MODD PowerPoint Design Tools toolbar to apply this green (the first color in the MODD design Classic Moss Green). Then, use the Transparency feature in the Colors dialog box (available through the More Fill Colors option on the Drawing toolbar's Fill Color pop-up menu) to match the effect you see here.

4. Add the shadow to the shape and use Shadow Settings to change the shadow's color. Notice that this color is the second color in the Classic Moss Green design, RGB (215,197,217).

5. Create the Lucerne text box in the same green as the Bevel shape, but without transparency.

6. Place the text box behind the shape (using the Order options on the Draw menu), and apply a shadow with the same shadow color that you applied to the Bevel shape.

7. Use the Nudge options on the Shadow Settings toolbar to move the text shadow directly above the shape's shadow, as you see here.

These two logos are both made from text created with the WordArt tool, combined with edited Clip Art.

Most Clip Art drawings can be ungrouped, and that provides you with a lot of additional content to work with! Here are a few pointers to help you do this effectively:

1. You may need to click Ungroup several times to fully ungroup the object.

2. Zoom in close to the object when ungrouping Clip Art and watch carefully as you delete elements, because elements of these drawings frequently overlap.

3. Don't be thrown if the object seems to ungroup into a million pieces! Just zoom in carefully and regroup the items you need as soon as you isolate them. Using the marquis method (click and drag around a group of objects to select them) comes in very handy here.

For example, I used a marquis to select the pieces of that book that ended up in the green logo above, then grouped them to extract the book from the original Clip Art. Then, I ungrouped it again to recolor it.

The images at right are the original Clip Art used to create the logos above.

In addition to deleting some pieces of this Clip Art and rearranging and recoloring some of the mountains, I used Edit Points to reshape the bottom of the mountains that fall at the front of my logo above.

Note: Please don't underestimate WordArt! This feature, available from the Drawing toolbar, might look like a kid's tool at first glance, but it's pretty powerful for creating artistic text. The character spacing and text border for the logo on the left are both features you can't get from regular text, and WordArt provides many options and much flexibility for getting just the right shape —such as for the logo on the right.

See the tip sheet "Creating and Editing Text Objects: Placeholders, AutoShapes, Custom Text Boxes and WordArt" for help with this often underutilized tool.

Edit Points is the feature used to create that funky L-shape for this logo. I particularly like the water-like flow because of the fact that the city of Lucerne, for which this company is named, has a very famous lake.

To create the text for *ucerne*, I started with a text box, cut it and pasted it back as a picture. Then, I just stretched the picture horizontally for the effect you see here.

To use Edit Points for objects such as this one:

1. Start with the Freeform tool (available from AutoShapes, Lines) and draw the basic idea of the shape you want in straight lines (just click to change direction when using the Freeform tool and double-click to end the drawing).

2. Then, right-click on the shape and select Edit Points.

In Edit Points, remember that you can right-click on any point to change the type of point (smooth point, corner point, etc.).

3. Drag the points as you like to alter the shape—it can be surprisingly fun, and provide great results, to just play a little bit without too much of a final result in mind. This is an extremely creative tool, and it's my favorite PowerPoint feature.

Check out the tip sheet on Edit Points referenced at the start of this chapter for detailed help with this cool tool.

These logos both use photographs from the Clip Art gallery. Remember that you can search for Clip Art and/or Photographs (as well as Movies and Sounds) using the Clip Art task pane.

Notice that the text of the logo on the left was created with WordArt—you can tell because the text has separate border and fill colors.

The text of the logo on the right was created as a text box, then I cut the text box and pasted it back as a picture, so that I could use the Brightness picture tool to fade the text color.

The only change from the original photo here is a bit of cropping, using the Crop tool on PowerPoint's Picture toolbar.

I cropped this photograph as well, and used the Brightness and Contrast picture tools to fade the image from the original.

Here are the original photographs used to create the above logos:

Next Steps and Quick Reference

Now that your creative juices are flowing, check out the next chapter to add some creativity and a professional edge to your everyday documents, such as letters and memos. We'll look at how to easily create your own brand image with a consistent, inspiring look for all of your documents—as well as how to make an impact by adding elements your audience might not expect to see in a basic document.

But first, check out the MODD designs and layouts demonstrated in this chapter.

MODD Designs Used in This Chapter

Sleek and Simple Black

Legacy Silver

True Blue Royal Blue

New Layouts Shown in This Chapter (and a Few Others): The MODD Full-Page Layouts

Bullets Over 2-Part Left, 3-Part Right

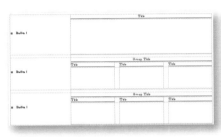

Bullets Left of Objects In 3 Rows, 1 Object Top, 3 Middle and Bottom

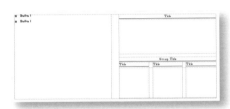

Bullets Left, 1 Object Over 3 Objects Right

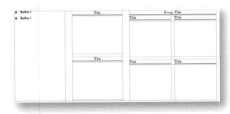

Bullets Left, 2 Parts Center, 4 Parts Right

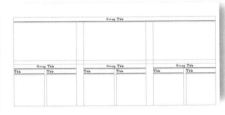

3 Parts Across Top, Each Over 2 Parts on Bottom

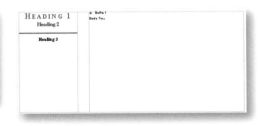

Left Page Headings, Bulleted Text Page

Left Page Headings: Object Page with 6 Parts

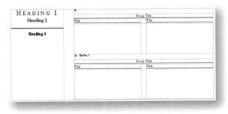

Left Page Headings: Text and Object Page with 4 Object Parts

Looking Your Sunday Best
Every Day: Creating basic documents that make a statement

Okay. You've explored the Microsoft Office tools at your disposal for making just the right statement with that landmark presentation or career-making report. But, what about the documents you create every day?

The luminous Jane Austen might not have had the ability to be unintelligible, but most of us have no problem being misunderstood or even occasionally overlooked—especially when it comes to the basic business communications we write all the time. And yet, without those 20 letters, memos, or faxes, we'd never get to that one landmark presentation! So, let's take a look at using Word, Excel, and PowerPoint for optimizing the effectiveness of every document you create, every day.

1. *Create letters that get to the point*
2. *Build not-so-basic memos*   **3.** *Create a brand image*   **4.** *Standardize design elements*   **5.** *Consider how your documents travel*

"I cannot speak well enough to be unintelligible." —Jane Austen

In this chapter, we'll address typical business documents with two goals in mind: using Word, Excel, and PowerPoint to help you communicate effectively and creating your own brand image for a consistent, professional, unique statement in every document.

Ever Thought of Donating That Memo to a Museum?

Think about the reasons you write a letter or memo. Regardless of what you do, you create a document because you have something to convey that's important enough to put in writing. You might be delivering information or requesting it, but the document's goal is always the same—the content of your document needs to be noticed, understood, and acted upon.

Take, for example, two versions of a simple business letter. The letters you see here contain exactly the same information:

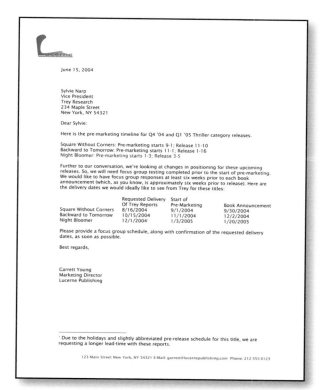

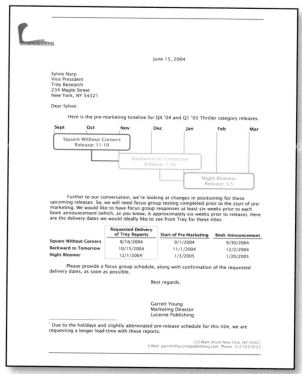

As you've seen in the document projects throughout this book, a *good* document is much more than a pretty face. What you see in the letter on the right, above, isn't about bells and whistles—it's about taking advantage of the tools available in the Office applications to help you communicate clearly, effectively, *and* brilliantly. Let's take a closer look at that letter.

The MODD Create a Doc tool automatically added my logo, contact information in the footer, and top and bottom page borders—as well as the styles for the indented letter format I selected.

Turning the unformatted table you saw in the other version of this letter into the one you see here takes just a minute, and look at the difference! It's clear, professional, and it draws focus to exactly what you need the reader to see.

Here's how to get it done:

1. Apply the appropriate paragraph styles from this document's MODD design (Emphatic Aquamarine)—Table Group Heading style is used for the column headings, along with Table Text style and Table Row Heading style, as appropriate.

2. Edit the Table Text style to include center paragraph alignment.

3. Select the second column and apply the coordinating cell border from Apply Design Color on the MODD Design And Layout toolbar.

Done!

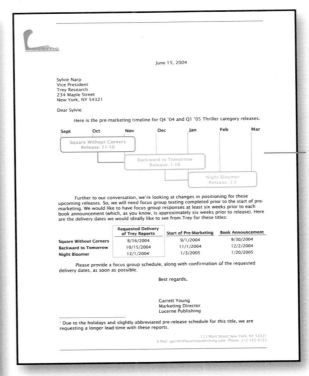

This is the same little flow chart you created at the beginning of the previous chapter. I've just made it smaller here so that it doesn't overpower the page.

This graphic replaces the three lines of text that provided the same information in the other version of this letter. Using a crisp and simple graphic here captures the reader's attention and clearly lays out information you want to have understood and utilized, rather than just read through.

Remember, the quality of a document doesn't mean how much color you add to it! Color, as you've seen throughout the projects in this book, is just a tool. Quality, when it comes to your documents, is about using the *best* tools to express *your particular document's content*.

Let's look at one more example. Here's a memo to a colleague providing staffing estimates over a five-month project period. You could just provide a laundry list of numbers—let him do his own number crunching! But take just a few minutes to chart that data and you add a volume of information that might be every bit as useful to you as to the person receiving it!

I started this document by using the Memo/Fax layout options from the MODD Create a Doc tool to select the page border, place my contact information in the header, and set up the single-column memo layout. Find the live version of this document in your *MODD Samples* folder, named *Lucerne – Memo.doc*.

Tip: If the recipient of your document might benefit from the detailed data that went into your chart—leave just the picture of your chart in the document (as you see it here), but send that Excel workbook along as an attachment. That way, your document focuses on what you want them to see, but they still get the detailed backup to reference on their own. What's more, if it is quantifiable data you're sending, they'll appreciate having it already waiting for them in Excel!

Remember that if you want the backup file to coordinate with your presentation (even when your presentation is just a memo), you can use MODD's Worksheet Design Colors tool to quickly apply your document's design colors to any worksheets (even the chart data) in the Excel workbook you're sending.

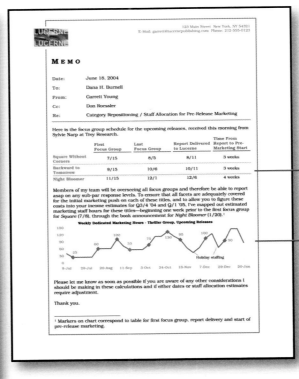

Use the Table Formatting tools on the MODD Doc Tools toolbar to apply the styles, borders, and cell margins on this table in a total of two clicks.

This Excel chart is a scatter line—I used that chart type to get the exact start and end dates I needed for the x-axis. I added the blue markers for the key dates by including an additional scatter series with no line.

Check out this chart and data setup for yourself. Find it in your *MODD Samples* folder, named *Lucerne – Staff Allocation Chart.xls*.

Of course, there is the short thank-you letter, or the fax confirming your receipt of that contract. Not every document benefits from charts, tables, and graphics. But *every* document can benefit from the consistent, professional look known as creating a *brand image*. And getting that done with Word, Excel, and PowerPoint is one of the easiest tasks we've taken on yet!

Brilliant Branding

A brand image. Perhaps you're thinking about your favorite clothing designer, or the brand of paper towel you buy, or maybe the logo on that can of soup Andy Warhol painted. But branding isn't just for products. Creating a brand image means creating your own unique impression—the statement you want your business communication to make about you. When it comes to any business, companies create their own branding for two principal reasons:

- A consistent look throughout all your written communications (documents, business cards, even your Web site) makes a solid, professional statement.

- A unique, well-crafted look gets you noticed and remembered.

Surely there's a color that reminds you of something whenever you see it—or a font that you identify with a product or company? That's branding. How about a celebrity with a well-crafted, unmistakable style? That's also branding. Whether you're a company or an individual, creating a brand image for your written communications can have a substantial impact on the impression you make.

Of course, large companies often have design firms to create their branding for them and celebrities have stylists and managers—but you have Microsoft Office! Each of the designs you've seen throughout this book could, for example, become our sample firm's branding. In fact, let's take a look at one additional branding concept for that same company and see just what type of document elements are part of the brand design.

Here, we see the same letter and memo from earlier in this chapter, using the Fresh Pumpkin MODD design, a coordinating logo, and a few consistent design elements. You can find these documents in your *MODD Samples* folder, called *Lucerne – Letter Brand.doc* and *Lucerne – Memo Brand.doc*.

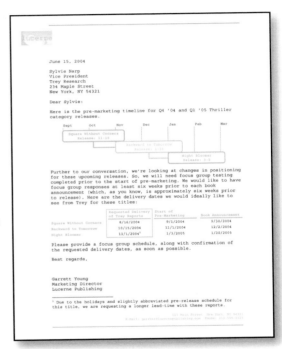

Elements of this brand's design:

✓ Logo

✓ Consistent colors

✓ Page borders

✓ The style, content, and placement of contact information

✓ Design elements, such as:

- left-aligned table headings with same-color paragraph borders

- heavy lines on charts and graphics

- a consistent color used for the axes in charts and graphics

This brand concept starts with a pre-created MODD Design. But, remember that the MODD designs are just jumping-off points to save you time—you can customize the styles, design colors, even the font and font size of your letters and memos. And, as for design elements to include in your branding—keep the quantity and content of design elements manageable for everyone who will be using your branding to create their documents.

The most important things in creating your brand identity are making design choices that you want to use to represent you (or your company) and selecting elements that can remain consistent throughout your documents.

Caution Take care not to overdo the standards you set up for your brand identity! Seventy or eighty paragraph styles, for example, are far too much to keep track of! Keep your design choices user-friendly and efficient. Branding should make it faster and easier to create documents, since you start documents having an idea of how they should look. Overwrought designs can make your document production efforts more complicated with less consistent results than using no branding at all!

Caviar Is Great, But It Doesn't Travel Well!

There is one more important element to keep in mind for your branding, and for every document you send: how the document will travel. The method of delivery can make a substantial difference in the features and formatting best used to create your document.

For the most part, you probably either e-mail, upload, mail, or personally deliver your documents—so how they look when printed and on screen is paramount. Well, you already have that covered—as you saw in Chapter 02, using Word, Excel, and PowerPoint's best practices can help you rest reasonably assured of what recipients will see when they open your document—whether they're opening an envelope or an e-mail attachment.

But what of photocopies and faxes? Consider the last logo we saw in the branding example. Nice logo—stylish, detailed, certainly unique.

Except, here's what it looks like when received by a typical fax machine:

Tip There's no need to stick to black and white when faxing or photocopying; if you want to be true to your branding—most vibrant colors fax and copy just as well! When creating your branding, fax a sample document to yourself so that you know which of your colors and design elements are best used in fax documents.

It's a great logo, but you might want to consider a second version of the logo that's more fax-worthy—something simple that has key elements in common with your primary logo (such as the font and, in this case, perhaps that crescent moon in the background image). Keeping it simple, and using bold colors that copy well in black and white, will present a more professional image and get your information across more effectively than the most exquisite logo or brilliantly conceived chart that becomes illegible at the other end of the fax line. Let's take a look at a couple of examples.

This fax version of the letter we looked at earlier in the chapter is almost identical to the original.

A simpler, easily readable version of your logo used just for fax documents adds a clean, professional touch. Notice that all other design elements remain true to my branding.

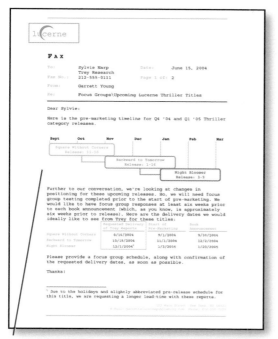

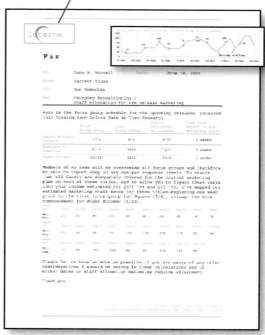

This fax has the same content as the memo you saw earlier in this chapter.

Sent by fax, that great-looking Excel chart above-left is too intricate to be read clearly. Instead, I'd go with a simple Word table of the data (as you see on the bottom half of this page), with text large enough to be readable when it reaches the other side of the fax line.

I used Edit, Paste Special, Transpose on the Excel data sheet to quickly turn the original chart data into the table configuration I needed for Word. Then all I had to do was copy the transposed data, paste it into Word and apply the styles. Find instructions for doing this in the referenced Excel file.

The only change in the body content is that I selected richer colors from my available brand colors for that flow chart. Deep, vibrant colors will transmit more accurately than pale colors, as you saw with the original logo for this brand.

Note: Check out the live version of the Excel data (*Lucerne – Staff Allocation Brand.xls*) to see the data for the table before it was pasted into Word.

Next Steps and Quick Reference

Regardless of the type of document you're creating, you've now had a look at using Word, Excel, and PowerPoint productively, efficiently, and for great-looking results. So where do you go from here? That's what the next chapter is going to tell you.

But first, check out the MODD designs and layouts demonstrated in this chapter.

MODD Designs Used in This Chapter

EMPHATIC AQUAMARINE

PUTTING GREEN

FRESH PUMPKIN

The MODD Letter, Memo, and Fax Layouts

Each time you create a letter, memo, or fax document using the MODD tools, you get several layout options that you can use to create your own brand image—or just to create a document that suits today's mood—in no more than a few clicks: select page borders, have your contact information added automatically to the document's header or footer, and choose a layout for your content.

Check out a few more combinations here in a variety of the MODD designs, and click the Get Started button on the MODD Main toolbar in Word for more detail on using the letter and memo/fax tools:

chapter 07

Next Steps:
You have the tools—now, make it your own!

What delights me the most about something so marvelous as this quote from Sartre is that it's just an *excerpt* from a *footnote*! And it's an interesting note indeed for the subject of this last chapter. The complete note (from Sartre's essay "What is Literature?") discusses how humans, in reality, are often consumed by the ends of their actions but, in poetry, the relationship is reversed.

So why talk about this here? Well, I'm not suggesting that your documents should resemble poetry. What I am suggesting is that—after you determine what you want your document to say—you take full advantage of the tools at your disposal throughout Microsoft Office by briefly reversing the relationship, as suggested by Mr. Sartre. Focus on what you can do in creating your document to make the

1. *Less really can be more* **2.** *Focus on the point of the page* **3.** *Go ahead and break the rules!* **4.** *Put it all together*

"The vase exists so that the girl may perform the graceful act of filling it; the Trojan War so that Hector and Achilles may engage in that heroic combat." —Jean-Paul Sartre

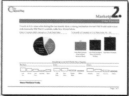

Note Find the live versions of these pages in your *MODD Samples* folder, named for the chapter and the corresponding sample page number in the order that you'll see them here (i.e., *Chapter 07 Page 1 Sample.doc*). The accompanying Excel and PowerPoint files are also available in that folder, and similarly named (though the PowerPoint elements for all four sample pages are combined into one file, *Chapter 07 PowerPoint.ppt*). You'll notice that the PowerPoint file contains the diagrams you'll see on these pages, as well as live versions of each logo.

Note Custom designs saved with the MODD tools are specific to each user. So, when you edit the documents I created with a custom design, the Apply Design Color dialog box in Word will not recognize the customized colors that were saved on my computer. Instead, select Change Design Association, accessible from the Apply Design menu on the MODD Design And Layout toolbar, to select a MODD Design or custom design of your own to associate with the document. No styles or other design elements currently in the document will be changed, but the Apply Design Color dialog box (as well as the Add Accent Shape tool on the MODD Doc Tools toolbar) will provide the colors from your newly associated design for the active document.

most effective statement on the page—simply, efficiently, and professionally—and make it distinctly yours, right down to the footnotes.

In this chapter, we'll revisit the document you saw at the beginning of this book (*Believe it or not.doc*, available in your *MODD Samples* folder). I've broken that document into separate pages so that we can look at four unique, customized approaches—from the design and layout to the choices about what stays on the page and how to best present it. Each of these pages improves upon something from the original document, resulting in a document that makes a stronger statement with its content, is equally solid to edit, and took even less effort to create than the original.

As you look at each of these pages, consider the most efficient methods for creating the various elements on the page, as well as what choices you might make differently if you were making the design and presentation choices here. Or just open up the live documents and customize them yourself—this is a great place to experiment with features and looks you want to try in your own documents.

Now, let's get to it!

For this document, I started with the Grand Cru Burgundy design, then edited paragraph styles and some of the design colors to create my own custom design.

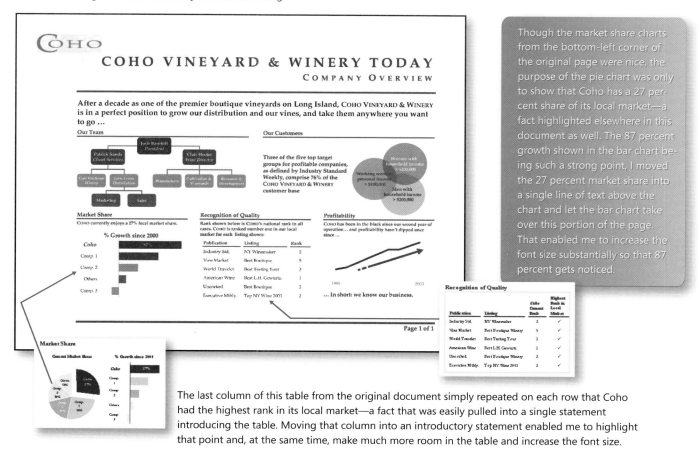

Though the market share charts from the bottom-left corner of the original page were nice, the purpose of the pie chart was only to show that Coho has a 27 percent share of its local market—a fact highlighted elsewhere in this document as well. The 87 percent growth shown in the bar chart being such a strong point, I moved the 27 percent market share into a single line of text above the chart and let the bar chart take over this portion of the page. That enabled me to increase the font size substantially so that 87 percent gets noticed.

The last column of this table from the original document simply repeated on each row that Coho had the highest rank in its local market—a fact that was easily pulled into a single statement introducing the table. Moving that column into an introductory statement enabled me to highlight that point and, at the same time, make much more room in the table and increase the font size.

As you see in that first sample page, some of the improvements I made in this version (over the original) were turning chart and table elements into paragraph text. Adding more graphics doesn't always make the document better. In fact, being selective about your graphics will help cement the focus of your pages. Take a look at the next page for another example of that.

The purpose of this page is to show how the wines that Coho focuses on are consistent with great, successful Old World wine regions and with the wines enjoying the fastest growing sales in the U.S. In the original page, however, those facts were buried in three small tables taking up the bottom third of the page. Drawn out into two simple, bold charts that are as fast and easy to create (if not more so) as the three little nested tables in the original—they completely refocus the page.

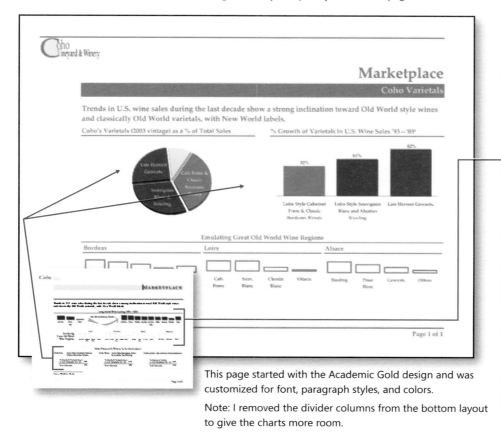

The graphic focus of the page in the original version showed the overall growth of Long Island winemaking, and its comparison to Old World regions. If this is information the recipient needs, it probably belongs in an appendix. Or, at the least, it should be secondary to the content that makes Coho stand out. By removing those charts and the graphic from the top of the page (none of which made specific reference to Coho) you get a much stronger page that was faster and easier to create than the original:

• 3D Pie chart and large column chart: five minutes each.

• Three small column charts (built by creating, sizing, and formatting the first, then duplicating to change the data): eight minutes for all three.

• Setting up this simple page layout using two of MODD's half-page layouts: no time at all!

This page started with the Academic Gold design and was customized for font, paragraph styles, and colors.

Note: I removed the divider columns from the bottom layout to give the charts more room.

Not sure how many graphical elements are too many? In the time I've spent in document production centers, I've seen no shortage of documents with 10 or 12 charts on a single page. Of course, to say that I've seen them is a bit misleading—nobody can actually *see* 12 charts on a page! At least, not without a helping hand from the Zoom command (or a good magnifying glass).

When I design a document, the most important question I ask is this: how can I make the reader *want* to read this page? Too often, people crowd their pages because there's so much important information to convey. But when pages are crowded, hard to read, and contain an overwhelming amount of content, they're likely to go unread entirely.

That said, there are ways to make space creatively. Just like those people who can fit an unimaginable amount of clothes in a small suitcase, make it look neat, and have it come out without any wrinkles (I've always admired them!), you can *create* space on the page. Remember, it only takes a minute to create a clean and unique table layout for organizing content in any number of ways. Go ahead and break the rules of traditional layout—you have the tools! Put key content in the heading area or let the page headings run down one side of the page. Use space creatively in whatever way works for *your* particular document and *your* particular style. Here's one example:

I customized the Elegant Lavender design for this document-giving it an entirely different feel from the original design just by altering a few of the design colors and changing the font.

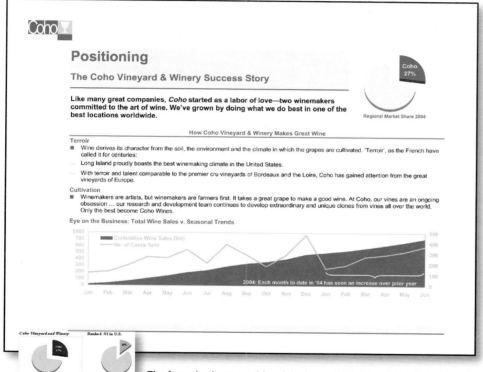

The top portion of this page is a simple one-row, two-column table—heading styles in the left cell and pie chart in the right. I liked this idea a lot, so I saved that table (along with the heading style paragraphs already in the left cell) as a custom layout.

It took just two minutes to create and save this unique layout. Then I can insert that custom layout to start every page in the document (or any document) and use the right-hand cell of the layout on each page for a different key graphic. (Notice that keeping the heading graphic simple is important to maintaining the clean feel of the page.)

The four pie charts on this original page highlighted Coho's local rank compared to the rankings of U.S. national leaders.

As with the previous sample page, taking away graphics that distracted from the most important points on the page provided more room for the information I most need to convey here.

All that considered, if you *must* have it all on the page (and we all know there are times when you must), be realistic about what can fit. Overburdening a page with too much content doesn't just overcomplicate the information in the document but the construction of it as well!

Keep in mind, as we discussed in the beginning of this book, that whether your important document is a simple letter or the presentation of your career—a well-constructed, well-organized document will help your content shine through. And it's *always* easier and faster to create than the alternative.

That brings us to our last sample page—a clean, well-organized (some might even say conservative) presentation page. But take a look—this page does everything a presentation page should do. It presents cohesive, well-organized information beautifully, in a solid document that will look good on any screen or out of any printer. The page takes advantage of Word, Excel, and PowerPoint's strong points to make the most of the content being delivered with the least amount of effort. The best part about this page? After the projects you've done throughout this book, you know how easy it is to create! Examine it for yourself. What went in to the making of this page?

Note When the four pages shown in this chapter are combined into one document, the file size ranges from 110 KB to 150 KB, depending on the design and logo chosen for the full document. That's even smaller than the original!

This page started with the Tried And True Navy Blue design. A few alterations in the colors and paragraph styles express a very different style of company than the original design implied.

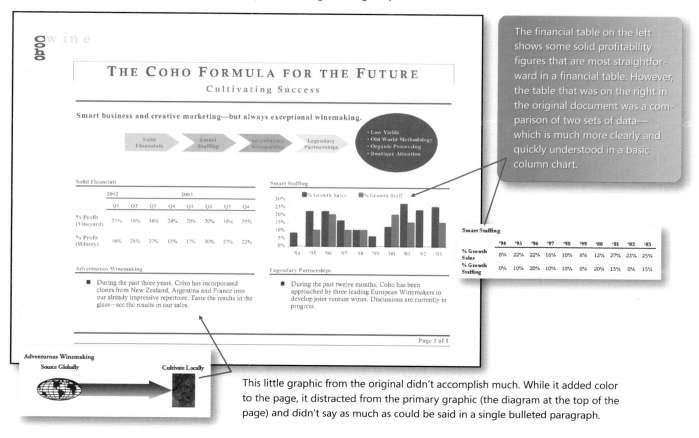

The financial table on the left shows some solid profitability figures that are most straightforward in a financial table. However, the table that was on the right in the original document was a comparison of two sets of data—which is much more clearly and quickly understood in a basic column chart.

This little graphic from the original didn't accomplish much. While it added color to the page, it distracted from the primary graphic (the diagram at the top of the page) and didn't say as much as could be said in a single bulleted paragraph.

A handful of paragraph styles, a couple of well-built tables, a few carefully chosen graphics, and you can transform any business communication into a document that speaks volumes!

Moving Forward

Note Don't forget to take advantage of the MODD tools as well to save time on every document—and reference the *How Do I...* articles and tip sheets whenever you need a hand with a new feature or a quick solution to a new document challenge. And keep this *Design Guide* handy for quick access to the *How Do I...* index and the design color guide.

You have the tools—now, make them your own!

So now that you're an Office document guru, remember that it's both about making great documents and making the time you spend in Office as productive as it can be! Take advantage of *every* tool Word, Excel, and PowerPoint have to offer your documents—from Word styles and tables to build solid documents quickly, to Excel data tools (like PivotTables) that help you put the best spin on your data and charts that show off that data's best side, to PowerPoint flow charts and diagrams that quickly and easily organize and highlight your key points. Let Office do the work; you have better things to do!

Isn't it nice to know that the less work you do, the better your documents will be—every time.

Appendix A
MODD Design Color Guide

The guide that follows provides the RGB (red, green, blue) values for the eight design colors associated with each of the 12 MODD Designs. These are the colors available in the Apply Design Colors dialog boxes in Word, Excel, and PowerPoint.

To apply the design colors from outside the Apply Design Colors dialog boxes, enter the RGB values (red, green, and blue values are separated by commas in the guide provided here) in the appropriate positions in the Colors dialog box for the Word, Excel, or PowerPoint feature you are using.

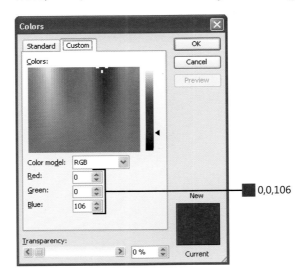

For most applicable features, the Colors dialog box can be accessed through the More Colors option (sometimes called More Line Colors, More Fill Colors, etc.) on Font, Border, Shading, Line, or Fill pop-up menus and drop-down lists throughout Word, Excel, and PowerPoint.

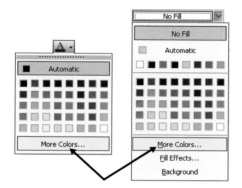

Note For Excel charts and work-sheets, note that colors are limited to the Excel color palette. When working in Excel on elements other than those accessible from the Drawing toolbar, apply MODD Design Colors through MODD's Chart Design Colors or Worksheet Design Colors features, or change the palette colors for the workbook through Tools, Options, Color. For help working with colors in Excel, see the article "Working with Colors: The Color Palette and Importing Colors from Other Files."

Tried and True Navy Blue

0,0,106   84,167,230   35,129,5   255,150,71   51,102,153   184,208,82   244,198,0   212,232,254

Classic Moss Green

0,60,0   215,197,217   145,168,213   228,234,231   255,255,204   255,165,165   200,252,246   204,204,255

Smashing Purple

91,22,116   232,162,86   196,86,112   97,135,102   70,40,120   226,181,120   255,181,181   234,203,245

Academic Gold

176,130,0   98,97,49   253,233,159   61,85,64   189,189,255   208,104,0   42,84,126   100,79,2

Elegant Lavender

125,55,149   89,149,90   255,220,149   244,234,248   90,0,90   232,176,176   145,172,247   252,168,0

Grand Cru Burgundy

122,0,56   172,127,0   152,128,128   90,45,0   100,144,174   203,161,173   104,110,0   222,209,176

Sleek and Simple Black

| 0,0,0 | 230,230,230 | 210,0,0 | 98,98,98 | 178,202,178 | 190,209,222 | 182,182,182 | 70,0,106 |

Legacy Silver

| 116,116,116 | 168,168,224 | 0,255,255 | 210,210,210 | 242,198,201 | 159,207,169 | 220,198,102 | 70,0,106 |

True Blue Royal Blue

| 4,19,164 | 200,0,0 | 225,220,0 | 25,200,25 | 255,175,0 | 0,0,110 | 153,0,153 | 200,200,200 |

Emphatic Aquamarine

| 0,108,172 | 255,184,27 | 157,133,255 | 123,207,62 | 227,237,19 | 174,150,150 | 0,64,122 | 204,141,0 |

Putting Green

| 37,170,10 | 255,255,0 | 67,98,255 | 154,198,50 | 246,169,212 | 255,174,55 | 62,129,21 | 240,240,120 |

Fresh Pumpkin

| 255,163,27 | 226,208,130 | 216,129,0 | 202,219,37 | 235,250,0 | 255,184,141 | 132,121,4 | 245,245,200 |

Appendix B
Troubleshooting the MODD Tools

If you experience difficulty while installing the MODD tools, or if you receive an error when using any feature of the MODD tools in Word, Excel, or PowerPoint, check out the topics that follow for quick solutions to common installation and usage issues.

Troubleshoot Installation

The Issue	The Solution	Tips and More Information
No new toolbars appear, or nothing happens when I click any MODD toolbar button in Word, Excel, or PowerPoint.	In the application experiencing the problem, confirm that Macro Security is set to Medium. To do this: 1. Go to Tools, Macro, Security. 2. On the Security Level tab of the Security dialog box, select Medium, then click OK. Close the application and then reopen. If the toolbars still do not appear or function correctly, see the troubleshooting steps in the next row of this table for Excel or PowerPoint, or the following row for Word.	Once the MODD tools are installed and running properly, increasing the Macro Security level will not stop them from running. However, it is important to set Security at Medium prior to installation, particularly for PowerPoint.

The Issue	The Solution	Tips and More Information
Macro Security is set to Medium, but toolbars in Excel or PowerPoint still do not appear or do not function.	These instructions will help you correctly load the MODD PowerPoint or Excel AddIn files. 1. Confirm that Macro Security (Tools, Macro, Security) is set to Medium in the application you are troubleshooting. For help getting this done, see the preceding table row. 2. In the affected application, go to Tools, Add-Ins. If you're in Excel, click the Browse button in the AddIns dialog box; if you're in Power-Point, click the Add New button in the AddIns dialog box. 3. Select the file for the appropriate application (MODD Excel or MODD PowerPoint) and click OK. If you are prompted with a dialog box warning about macros, click the Enable Macros option. Click OK or Close to close the Add-Ins dialog box. Your toolbars should now be present and function normally.	If the files MODD PowerPoint or MODD Excel do not appear when you take these steps, use the Repair option in the MODD Installer to repair and complete your installation. The next row of this table will help you access the Repair tool.

The Issue	The Solution	Tips and More Information
The MODD toolbars in Word, Excel, or PowerPoint are missing or do not function after taking the steps in the preceding row(s).	Important: Before running the Repair option described here, take note of the RGB values for the custom colors saved with any of your custom designs, as these may be deleted during repair. Other custom settings (designs, layouts, or logo) you have saved with the MODD tools, and any files in the *MODD Samples* folder that you have changed, will remain in tact. 1. Insert the MODD CD and select Troubleshooting from the main menu. 2. Click the option to run Setup. 3. When prompted by the installer with the options to Modify, Repair, or Remove the installation, click Repair. The installer will repair your installation, replacing and loading files as needed.	The Repair feature will replace any missing files and correct the installation of the MODD tools in any application that was experiencing a problem. Note: If custom design colors are lost during repair, select Manage, Edit A Custom Design from the Custom Designs And Layouts menu on the MODD Design And Layout toolbar. You can re-enter your custom colors in the second step of that tool.
Another user of my computer installed MODD, but I have no access to it.	MODD is installed individually for each user of the computer. Follow the installation steps in the first chapter of this book, or from Install Microsoft Office Document Designer on the main page of the MODD CD.	Important: Some files are shared between multiple users of MODD on the same computer. If one user wants to remove MODD, but other users of the same computer will continue to use the MODD tools, see the last row of this table for important information.

The Issue	The Solution	Tips and More Information
The MODD tools run slowly, or they freeze or crash one or more applications when used.	Please review the recommended minimum system requirements for running the MODD tools, which you can find in Chapter 00.	
I want to remove the MODD tools from my computer.	In Control Panel (accessible from the Windows Start menu), open Add or Remove Programs. In the list of currently installed programs, select MODD, and then click Remove.	Caution: Manually deleting files instead of using the Remove feature on the installer might not remove all MODD files and settings, and might cause problems for other users of the same computer who are still running MODD.
I am one of multiple users of MODD on the same computer and want to remove the tools just from my user account.	When multiple users of the same computer are using the MODD tools, remaining users may need to replace some files if one user removes the tools. 1. Prior to any user removing the MODD tools, all users on the same computer should take note of the RGB values of any custom colors saved with custom designs. 2. Then, if any errors are experienced after one user removes MODD, any other user can run the Repair feature accessible from the Troubleshooting section available on the start page of the MODD CD.	Note: If saved custom design colors are lost after running the Repair feature, go to Manage, Edit a Custom Design, available from the Custom Designs and Layouts menu on the MODD Design And Layout toolbar to re-save your custom color values with the applicable design(s).

Troubleshoot Using the MODD Tools

The Issue	The Solution	Tips and More Information
I see an error message saying that required files are missing when I try to use one or more of the features on the MODD toolbars.	Important: Before running the Repair option explained here, take note of the RGB values for the custom colors saved with any of your custom designs, as these may be deleted during repair. Other custom settings (designs, layouts, or logo) you have saved with the MODD tools, and any files in the *MODD Samples* folder that you have changed, will remain in tact. 1. Insert the MODD CD and select Troubleshooting from the main menu. 2. Click the option to run Setup. 3. When prompted by the installer with the options to Modify, Repair, or Remove the installation, click Repair. The installer will repair your installation, replacing and loading files as needed.	Deleting or moving *any* files in the following locations will cause some or all of the MODD tools to be unable to function: ■ C:\Document Designer or its subfolders ■ Your Word, Startup folder ■ Your Microsoft, AddIns folder Note: If custom design colors are lost during repair, select Manage, Edit A Custom Design from the Custom Designs And Layouts menu on the MODD Design And Layout toolbar. You can re-enter your custom colors in the second step of that tool.

The Issue	The Solution	Tips and More Information
Using the Repair feature of the MODD installer did not resolve my issues.	You will need to uninstall and reinstall the MODD tools. Before doing this, move any files from your *MODD Samples* folder that you have altered or created yourself and would like to save. Then: 1. In Control Panel, open Add or Remove Programs. 2. In the list of currently installed programs, select MODD, and then click Remove. 3. After the installer completes the process of removing your installation, you can return to the MODD CD, select Install Microsoft Office Document Designer, and follow the installation wizard provided to properly install the MODD tools.	Important: If you are going to remove and reinstall MODD, confirm that Macro Security is set to Medium in Word, Excel, and PowerPoint, and close all three applications—as well as Microsoft Outlook—before reinstalling.
The results I get when I use a particular feature of the MODD tools seem to be wrong.	Please consult the Get Started document for the application containing the feature you would like to troubleshoot. The Get Started documents provide an overview of each of the features available in the MODD tools. You can access the Get Started document either by clicking the Get Started button on the MODD toolbars in Word, Excel, or PowerPoint, or through the Introduction option available from the MODD CD main menu.	If you are unfamiliar with any Word, Excel, or PowerPoint feature discussed in the Get Started documents, use the *How Do I...* index in this book to find the topic you need, and then access the referenced *How Do I...* articles and tip sheets from the MODD toolbars in Word, Excel, and PowerPoint.

The Issue	The Solution	Tips and More Information
Part of the *How Do I...* documents are cut off when printed.	For best results when printing *How Do I...* documents, change the page orientation to landscape. To do this in Internet Explorer: 1. Go to File, Page Setup. 2. Select Landscape from the Orientation options, and then click OK.	You will see no difference when viewing the articles in your Web browser after changing the page orientation, but the pages will print in landscape orientation—allowing all content to print.
The *How Do I...* documents are difficult to read or missing images.	If you did *not* delete any files in C:\Document Designer, this might be a result of compatibility issues with your Web browser. If you are unable to view the articles and tip sheets completely in your Web browser, try saving the document to a location of your choice (use File, Save As from your Web browser), then open the document using File, Open in Word. All *How Do I...* documents are HTML files.	Make sure that you have Internet Explorer 5.0 or later installed for best results when viewing the *How Do I...* articles and tip sheets.

Index to *How do I...* Content

See also Index for book content.

Index

See also Index to How do I...content.

documents, *continued*
creating space on a page, 130
incorporating Excel charts, 69–89
adding pictures to, 91–110
building presentation pages, 51–66
creating tables, 55–59
nesting tables, 59–63
organizing pages, 52–55
creating presentation pages, 132–133
delivering, 119–121
faxing, 119–121
formatting marks, 34
impeccability, 32–35
photocopying, 119–121
drawing connectors, 95

E

edits, undoing and redoing, 16–21
Excel, 43–46
adding numbers, 30–32
charts
applying colors to, 137
displaying data, 75–81
displaying legends, 84
incorporating into documents, 69–89
resizing, 44–45
using PivotCharts, 79
using PivotTables, 75–79
using scatter charts, 82–84
vs. Word and PowerPoint, 43
performing mathematical calculations, 46
spreadsheets vs. Word tables, 43

F

faxing documents, 119–121
flow charts, adding to documents, 96–99, 114
fonts, 39
formatting
fonts, 39
levels of, 39–42
paragraphs, 40
sections, 41
shortcuts, 22–23
marks, 34
defined, 34
turning on, 36
presentation graphics, 47

G

graphics
adding to documents, 91–110
adding flow charts, 96–99, 114
creating logos, 104–108
enhancing appearance of graphics, 93–108
using AutoShapes, 95, 96, 101, 106–108
adding to pages, 130–132
creating space on a page, 130
presentation, 47

H

host (outside) tables, 59, 60, 63, 64
How Do I... documents, finding information in, 12–13

I

impeccability of documents, 32–35
inserting objects and shapes, 10
inside (nested) tables, 59–64
creating, 60
formatting and sizing, 62
installing MODD tools, 7–8
removing MODD tools, 144
repairing installation, 145–146
troubleshooting installation, 141–144

L

layouts
organizing, in pages, 55–67
using to create brand images, 122–123
legends, displaying, 84
levels of formatting in Word, 39–42
font formatting, 39
paragraph formatting, 40
section formatting, 41
logos
creating with PowerPoint, 104–108
relationship to document delivery, 119–121

About the Author

Stephanie Krieger is a document production expert with more than a dozen years of computer experience—the past nine of which she has spent as a consultant specializing in Microsoft Office documents. She has helped many global companies develop enterprise solutions for their Office products, taught hundreds of professionals and dozens of professional software trainers to build great documents by understanding the way that Office applications "think," and developed customized document solutions for clients utilizing Microsoft Visual Basic for Applications and XML for the Office System. Stephanie is both a technical writer and a fiction writer, as well as a serious student of 18th century philosophy. She publishes a Weblog at arouet.net, where you can find Office tips and discuss philosophers from the Enlightenment era. You can also contact Stephanie via e-mail at MODD_2003@msn.com. *Microsoft Office Document Designer* is Stephanie's first book.

What do you think of this book?
We want to hear from you!

Do you have a few minutes to participate in a brief online survey? Microsoft is interested in hearing your feedback about this publication so that we can continually improve our books and learning resources for you.

To participate in our survey, please visit:
www.microsoft.com/learning/booksurvey

Enter this book's ISBN, 0-7356-2037-7. As a thank-you to survey participants in the United States and Canada, each month we'll randomly select five respondents to win one of five $100 gift certificates from a leading online merchant.* At the conclusion of the survey, you can enter the drawing by providing your e-mail address, which will be used for prize notification *only*.

Thanks in advance for your input. Your opinion counts!

Sincerely,

Microsoft Learning

Learn More. Go Further.

To see special offers on Microsoft Learning products for developers, IT professionals, and home and office users, visit: *www.microsoft.com/learning/booksurvey*